The RESEARCH REPORT

A GUIDE FOR THE BEGINNER

By

ELLEN JOHNSON

DEPARTMENT OF ENGLISH
PURDUE UNIVERSITY

THE RONALD PRESS COMPANY ⸱ NEW YORK

PREFACE

This manual presents a simplified procedure for introducing the inexperienced student to the essentials of research. Although there are no "three easy lessons" that will prepare the novice to conquer the complexities of advanced research, he can nevertheless learn the essentials of investigation, compilation, quotation, and documentation, and how to do them accurately. It is these, then, and the simpler mechanics of research, that are covered in this introduction. Nothing more is attempted. While designed particularly for use by the college student in conjunction with his work in English composition, this brief guide should be of equal value wherever training in the earliest stages of research is undertaken.

Although there are accepted variants in the procedures and mechanics of research, I have respected the request of one student who said, "Don't teach us more than one way to do a thing when we are doing it the first time. We can always adapt ourselves in the future after we have learned one right way of doing it." This is the first of four general principles which I have found effective in my classes and so have relied upon in the preparation of this material. The others are described in the three following paragraphs.

The correct use of the mechanics of research is achieved more rapidly and effectively when the mechanics themselves are subordinated to their proper place in the whole undertaking. Attention should be focused upon the spirit of the investigation and the problem of presenting the results to the reader. This subordination of the mechanics allows the placing of emphasis where it belongs: upon their function and upon the economy of time and effort that results from their use. This, of course, boils down to the single essential, that the student must understand the need for mechanics and how the accepted conventions fulfil that need.

Students learn more readily and with more enthusiasm by

emulation of their peers; thus examples are most effective when they are supplied from the writings of other underclassmen. As the average freshman has had almost no experience with documented writing when he begins his research paper, these models should include a variety of types.

The objective is not just to bring the student to a point where he can write one paper correctly, but to where he writes the kind of paper that will prepare him to write other papers.

The text is liberally illustrated with examples of student research, all of which were written by undergraduates in my classes at Purdue University. The papers have been carefully selected not only to provide the necessary variety, but also to meet certain specific needs. For instance, such papers can be particularly useful in helping to overcome the prevailing fault among inexperienced researchers of making a "patchwork quilt" when putting together their data. The Carson paper, alone, is an excellent model for this purpose. As this fault can be over-corrected, the Hart paper should serve as an antidote. Finally, the last four papers have been particularly chosen because they highlight respectively essential points of documentation, compilation, investigation, and quotation.

The student papers are presented essentially as they were written. Their special merits in each case are explained. If in other respects they have imperfections, the student may profit by them. A model need not be perfect to be useful as an illustration.

I am grateful to my students, not only to those whose writings appear in this text, but also to the many others whose cooperative response and whose trials and errors have determined the development of the material in its present form. Especially am I grateful to my department head, Dr. Herbert LeSourd Creek, whose encouragement has brought this text to completion.

Lafayette, Indiana
June, 1950

ELLEN JOHNSON

CONTENTS

I. ASSIGNMENTS AND ILLUSTRATIONS

II. MODELS AND ADAPTATIONS

I
ASSIGNMENTS AND ILLUSTRATIONS

A

THE DOCUMENTED MANUSCRIPT

Before even beginning the research study, the student should have a clear understanding of the requirements of a documented manuscript. Many manuscripts must be documented that are not research papers at all. Documentation is required whenever material from reading is used in writing. The general rule is this: for every *quotation,* every *distinctive phrase,* every *piece of information,* every *idea taken from reading,* the reader should be able to find the *page* of the exact source the writer has read.

Exact source can only be provided through citing a specific page in a particular publication. Before the reader can find that particular page, he must know the name of the *author,* the *title* of the book or article, the name of the *publisher or publication,* and the *date* it appeared in print. These make up the *bibliographical description,* which must be given at some point in the paper. If the paper has a bibliography, the description may be condensed elsewhere in the paper; but if the paper has no bibliography, all the necessary description must be given at the point where the source is first mentioned.

Obviously this can make writing difficult. The writer must of course make clear *in any paragraph* when observations or opinions are taken from other writers, but it would make dreary reading if he had to load the paragraph with all the bibliographical details for every item borrowed. It is to relieve such deadliness that the footnote convention is invented as an economy.

Much documented writing, even in publication, is dull and difficult reading, partly because it does not sufficiently point out the significance of the data presented, and partly because the

3

necessary acknowledgment of sources is so laboriously introduced as to impede the reading. The Carson report (appearing
on pages 66-80) is evidence that both these defects can be
avoided, even when the explanatory statement goes to considerable length. Carson's paper will furnish many hints as to
how difficulties can be overcome and a readable paper presented.

In a less formal paper than Carson's, the footnoting may be
reduced to much greater economy. Just be sure that the reader
can find the page.

A Few Cautions on Documenting

1. *Dates.* Care should be taken in presenting material from
sources published at different times. The researcher must take
account of the time element. If a writer of 1923 says something
is "at present" true, the student citing the information must not
say that it is "at present" true, but rather that it was said to be
true in 1923.

2. *Ideas.* Unless otherwise indicated, the *ideas* presented by
the student are presumed to be his own. Even when he is in
agreement with the author cited, the *wording of the paragraph*
must indicate when the conclusions, opinions, advice, or observations have their source in other writings.

3. *Summaries.* When summaries of extended passages are
introduced, the "according to whom" should be stated at the
beginning. If the summary extends to several paragraphs, the
continuity of reference should be made clear with each new
paragraph. The footnote reference can conclude the passage or,
if the symbol has been placed earlier, the wording must indicate
when the discussion reverts to the ideas of the writer of the
paper.

4. *Quotations.* Indiscriminate quotation is to be avoided.
One quotes because the point is particularly well expressed or
because he wishes to repeat the statement exactly as it appeared
in the source. In introducing the quotation the connection, both

to context and source, should be made clear in the wording of the paragraph. Rarely is it sufficient to use quotation marks and the symbol referring to the footnote. At least say "as so and so puts it."

When quoting indirectly, if John said, "I am going down town," one need not say that John said he was "going down town." If, however, John said, "I am peregrinating toward the village," it would be better to say that John said he was "peregrinating" toward the village.

A passage quoted verbatim may either be placed in the paragraph within quotation marks or be blocked in the text (single spaced in typing) without quotation marks. N.B. No matter how lacking in distinction the style, it is not satisfactory practice to copy passages from books and merely put the footnote symbol. The paragraph should show that they are presented as the statements of other writers.

When the footnote symbol appears *without* any source reference in the wording of the text, the reader assumes that all the *facts,* or the *information,* back to the first break (the beginning of the paragraph, or a preceding footnote symbol within the paragraph) is from the source indicated. Where this is not the case, the source reference must be brought into the wording of the text at the point where the borrowed information is introduced.

What is note and what is comment should always be perfectly clear from the wording of the paragraph. (See Carson's use of his notes 6 and 7, page 71.) Conversely, if you are referring to something from memory, do not pretend to document it! Treat it as part of your general information (note Sanders' reference to Edison, page 11). At best it is something you "read somewhere."

Assignment A

Write a two-page paper *presenting your own ideas* but introducing several references to reading. For best results it is recommended that you try to bring in at least one direct quotation and at least one reference presenting the facts or ideas in your own words.

This assignment is short enough that it should be rewritten until it is correct in all essentials.[1]

1. If it is merely faulty mechanically, make the indicated corrections and present a fresh copy.
2. Does the wording of the paragraph need revision to connect the ideas and show the proper relation to source?
3. Are the borrowed units well related to the composition as a whole, or should the theme be rewritten?
4. Perhaps the theme idea was not a good one for the purpose of the assignment. In that case it might be easier just to write another theme.

If after rewriting you do not make a satisfactory grade on this assignment, you should have a conference with your instructor before attempting Assignments B3 and B4. This is a very important assignment. Once it is mastered, you should have little difficulty with the remaining assignments.

The student themes which follow were written in fulfilment of this assignment. The Sanders paper, included among the following, in its first form brought in references in the student's own words, as the assignment suggests. In revising the paper to give it a better unity, Sanders happened to retain only the direct quotations. The revised version is presented here. The other papers are presented in their original form.

---

[1] This is one paper which is not graded until the copy is as it should be. This is the assignment in which the student masters the mechanics. In the criticism of the paragraphs, conferences may be needed to determine what is the student's general information and what he has read for the paper.

ILLUSTRATIONS OF ASSIGNMENT A

IT'S NOT SO BAD AS HE THINKS

by James E. Blythe

The May issue of the Atlantic Monthly contains an article by David L. Cohn entitled "Who Will Do the Dirty Work?"[1] The general theme of the article is that today in the United States you cannot "rise above your station" to any great extent.[2] The author tries to show that men prefer to do "white collar" work rather than manual labor; and, as a result, they are frustrated in their desires when, because of a lack of opportunity, they must run a lathe instead of an office.[3]

In general, I agree with this conclusion; however, I do not agree with some of the assumptions used to prove it. In this paper I should like to reveal these differences of opinion and tell why I disagree with Mr. Cohn on some of his points.

"The modern man and the modern woman hate physical work."[4] This statement seems to be partly true; but, nevertheless, we hate mental work to an even greater extent. How many wage earners bother to make out their own income tax—or are even able to? How many women stop to add up the grocery bill or to count their change? Yes, we hate physical work; but somehow we endure it because we have to. Mental work, however, is something that we can completely ignore or else pay someone to do for us. For this reason I cannot agree

---

[1] Vol. 183, No. 5 (May, 1949), pp. 45-48.

[2] P. 46.

[3] P. 48.

[4] P. 45.

with Mr. Cohn that man prefers to do mental labor. You are more likely to see a man doing the physical labor of spading a garden at home than the mental work of making out a budget or calculating his fuel bill for the past winter.

"Suppose you say to ... a garbage collector ... that he ought to rise above his station, and he cannot do it?" [5] What does Mr. Cohn consider to be above his station—teaching school? In my home town, uneducated garbage collectors are paid more than college educated school teachers. Does the author mean to indicate that the local garbage collector would be happier if he were one of the intelligentsia and earning less? I think not. And who looks down upon this man? Certainly not the underpaid school teacher.

Mr. Cohn feels that it is commonly thought that "physical labor is not respectable." [6] I have more often heard the phrase that "he has never worked a day in his life," than the one that "physical labor is not respectable." Any engineer graduating today certainly must respect the laborer earning nearly twice what he is. This should also hold true for the graduates in other fields. If salary is the basis for respect, then the college graduate is the one who should be looked down upon and not the laborer.

Mr. Cohn is right when he says that a laboring job does not command the respect that a white collar job does; but it is not so bad as he thinks.

------

[5] P. 47.

[6] P. 48.

JOHN L. LEWIS'S COAL STRIKE

by John P. Ryan

Since November no man, except possibly the President, has had his name in the papers more often than John L. Lewis. The reason is that Mr. Lewis has had the members of his United Mine Workers Union out on one of their longest and most costly strikes. What are some of the reasons behind this strike that has caused Mr. Lewis's name to appear in print so much, and how will the differences be settled?

Mr. Lewis has several reasons for this long strike. As a recent issue of U. S. News and World Report reported, "John L. Lewis is not happy about his 1949 record of getting things for the miners of coal. . . . the miners have suffered sharp loss of income this year [1949] and have little to show in the way of added benefits for the year ahead." [1] Consequently, Mr. Lewis will first demand higher wages. The pay of the miners, as a group, has increased as much as the pay of any other group, but the increased living costs have eaten most of these increases right up. This same magazine pointed out in another issue that the pay scales have risen from $9.05 per day to $14.05 per day, but that these increases have been met by increased living costs. [2]

A second demand is for increased payment to the welfare fund. The fund was financed at the start solely by the operators, who paid

---

[1] "Whispers," U. S. News and World Report, Vol. 27, No. 20 (November 11, 1949), p. 68.

[2] "High Cost of Strikes," U. S. News and World Report, Vol. 27, No. 16 (October 14, 1949), p. 11.

a royalty of five cents a ton on coal, but the royalty was increased to twenty cents a ton.[3] Mr. Lewis has asked that since the fund is almost defunct the royalties be raised to thirty cents a ton; also, that the board of trustees be changed, especially the representative for the operators.

Mr. Lewis has asked for other terms. These terms include a seven hour day, instead of the present eight hour day, and the continued maintenance of the "able and willing" clause of former contracts.

As a last item, Mr. Lewis would like to discredit the Taft-Hartley Law. Mr. Truman, who is also opposed to the law, delayed using the law and thus skillful maneuvers by Lewis have brought the law to its severest test. Mr. Truman's disdain for the act kept him from invoking the law, and when he finally did use it, it backfired and the law was not effective at all. Regarding the use of the Taft-Hartley Law, Mr. Henry Hazlitt points out in Newsweek, "By the time he [Mr. Truman] did, our national economic life was already in such peril that John L. Lewis could dictate any terms he pleased." [4] This tends to show that Lewis has already won at least one of his points.

These demands and attempts on the part of Mr. Lewis have made him one of the most written about men in the past year. I have tried to point out some of his requests, but it is almost impossible to obtain all the details which the operators and Mr. Lewis have argued over. When the strike is over, many of these points will be made clear to the consumer public.

─────

[3] Ibid., p. 13.

[4] Henry Hazlitt, "The Needless Crisis in Coal," Newsweek, Vol. 35, No. 10 (March 6, 1950), p. 68.

THE VALUE OF INSIGHT

by Dorian H. Sanders

Thomas A. Edison was a great man and a great benefactor to humanity. He gave the world much through his tireless investigation. Edison, however, was not a theoretical man: he was a practical man. He neither worked from theory nor developed any. He was not a scientist but an inventor. Edison's great attributes were his curiosity, his patience, and his keenness of eye and mind. Many of his discoveries resulted from a methodical trial and error process, but most of them resulted from sheer accident. It was his perception and quickness to interpret the results of these accidents that made him the great man that he was.

The value of such insight in scientific investigation was recognized long before Edison, but far too few had developed this faculty. One scientist recently wrote, "Long ago Pasteur recognized that when accident favors an investigator it [the accident] must be met by sharp insight, for he uttered the wise and discerning dictum, 'Dans les champs de l'observation, le hasard ne favorise que les esprits préparés.' Even before Pasteur, Joseph Henry, the American physicist, enunciated the same truth when he said, 'The seeds of great discoveries are constantly floating around us, but they only take root in minds well prepared to receive them.' " [1]

Thus seeing is psychological as well as physiological. The mind must contribute an idea of what is seen—and what the mind contributes

---

[1] Walter B. Cannon, "Gains from Serendipity," College Prose, edited by Theodore F. Gates and Austin Wright (2nd ed.; Boston: D. C. Heath & Co., 1946), p. 205.

depends largely on the training and background of the individual.

Research is carried on today by highly trained men and women. Their minds are trained to observe details and to grasp the significance of their experimentation. Their minds are amply fertile for the seeds of discovery to take root. Although research today is carried out on a more scientific basis using a logical approach to the subject, this does not mean that discoveries by accident no longer happen; on the contrary, researchers are even quicker to seize upon their happy accidents.

Modern science, indeed, should agree with the Apostle Paul, who wrote, "Finally, brethren, whatsoever things are true, whatsoever things are honest, whatsoever things are just, whatsoever things are pure, whatsoever things are lovely, whatsoever things are of good report; if there be any virtue, and if there be any praise, think on these things." [2]

Thus, in other words, to see truth, honesty, or beauty, we must have mental activity of our own which is receptive to such things. The modern researcher, as did Edison, must develop a keen eye and a keen mind.

-----

[2] Phil. 4:8.

B

THE RESEARCH PAPER

This assignment is a brief study of a special type, designed to provide an easy check on the student's procedure and help the beginner over the tricky places with the least expenditure of time and effort. The project is broken down into four easy stages; they form, however, one continuous process culminating in the report described in part four.

1. The Subject for a Research Paper

An enjoyable and valuable part of research training is the finding of a subject. Yet this can be difficult for the beginner. There are many new subjects to be discovered in existing books, but generally experience is required to find them. How is the beginner, without a specialist's knowledge, to discover what is new in a field unless he does a great deal of preliminary reading? There is one safe short cut for a first try at research.

One may suppose that the articles appearing in reputable general magazines reflect current topics and present discussions that the average reader can understand. Such subjects furnish the principle of classification in the *Readers' Guide to Periodical Literature*. If in recent issues of the *Readers' Guide* one can find six titles which suggest a seventh not yet written, he can be reasonably sure that he is on the way to a good research study.

This approach is suggested for several additional reasons:

1. The beginner should have an introduction to such indexes and bibliographical guides, and to their incidental as well as their designed values.
2. He may discover fresh interests in subjects which had not occurred to him independently.

3. He should discover how valuable bibliographical description is as a clue to content, how much can be learned of what is written before actually reading it at all, how titles may suggest authorities and subtopics to guide the investigation.

The investigator should consider all details of the bibliographical description. There are important clues in dates, in the length of articles, in the types of periodicals, in the names of authors, and of course in the wording of the titles themselves, individually and in comparison.

Assignment B1

Go to the very recent issues of the *Readers' Guide* and discover three subjects which might be suitable for research, and report them to the class. Present your analysis of the titles and suggest what might be done. Point out some subtopics or other leads suggested in the titles that might ultimately build up into a plan. Suggest an approach. Be sure that the titles selected are interrelated to focus upon a central point of interest.

Even at this early stage it is advisable to form the habit of separating the notes of a compilation. Each title is a separate unit. Record each on a separate 3″ × 5″ card.[2]

As an illustration, the following subjects led to good research studies in the spring of 1949: meteorites, water fowl, Pan-American Highway, television transmission, alcoholism, the Taft-Hartley Act, solar heating of houses, the "Coup d'Etat" in Syria, teachers: supply and demand, Axis Sally, consolidation of schools.

Written Report. Summarize your oral report in a brief written report:

---

[2] Mechanical details are not of first importance at this stage. For those who wish the practice of having things in good form, there is an illustration in the Appendix, p. 122, and the form is discussed in the next assignment, p. 17.

1. List the three subjects as precisely worded as you can.
2. Under each, state what you would hope to find out in reference to what the titles promise that you can find out.
3. Enclose the title cards in evidence that your conclusions are reasonably drawn.

2. The Bibliography of a Study

A study is not a good study if it is not based on the best sources available. To make a judicious selection, therefore, one must know all the sources available. Consequently, even a brief study begins with a complete bibliographical investigation. A complete investigation does not mean the indiscriminate collection of a vast number of titles vaguely related to the subject; it means a selective process of discovering what is related to the point in question.

One may collect fifty titles and use only six. But before he collects a hundred titles he should take stock and ask himself if he really knows what he is driving at. Is the subject too broad, too vague? Can he set a time limit from which he can bring the study up to date? He should not rest on mere quantity and quit, but should restrict his selection for a reason. Further, he should continue to scrutinize the titles he has selected and alter his plan accordingly.

But when he has finished, the investigator should have recorded, each on a 3″ × 5″ card, every available source that he might wish to use in his inquiry. Some of these he may read no further than the bibliographical description. These he will ultimately place in the supplementary bibliography of his report, thus permitting the reader to evaluate his selection of sources actually used in the study.[3]

But the researcher does not decide at this stage what to leave *unread*. Presumably anything in the bibliography might be

---

[3] These bibliographic divisions are discussed in Assignment B4, pp. 27 f. They do not concern our present purpose, which is to determine the order of reading for the best approach to the study.

referred to, or it should not be there. He begins by selecting what is of *first* importance to *read*. Which titles are most general, suggesting the quickest approach to an understanding of the subject as a whole? Do any names stand out as possible authorities in the field? Do some of the periodicals seem more readable, some of the articles of better length?

When the bibliography is completed, the study should, for the purposes of the present assignment, meet the following tests:

1. Is the subject timely and up-to-date, with important publicity in recent months?
2. Is the bibliography of manageable magnitude—enough to permit thorough study without too much reading?
3. Is the problem definite, with suggested subpoints for note taking?
4. Will the report be a contribution to the field, its findings not covered in any one previous source?

Assignment B2

Select a subject of your own discovery or one suggested in the class,[4] and compile a complete bibliography of the sources available in the library. Consult the card catalog for material on your subject or its subtopics. Consult the older issues of the *Readers' Guide* as far back as your study requires. (Take care not to leave out any issues for the period you are considering.) Consult the encyclopedias for articles on your subject. (Be sure to note the editions of such reference works: the *Encyclopaedia Britannica* is now in its fourteenth edition, for example, but the eleventh is still valuable.) If your problem is a special one, consult the reference librarian for guidance to more specialized sources of information.[5]

---

[4] Before you go any further, it might be well to glance over the current articles to be sure that they contain the kind of material you can use.

[5] Some additional reference works are listed in the Appendix, pp. 119 ff.

Record each title on a 3″ × 5″ card. For convenience of later reference the bibliographical description is separated into three lines:

the author
the title
the facts of publication

The author's surname is placed first, for ready reference. The name of the document appears in italics. In typescript or manuscript this is indicated by underscoring. Quotation marks set off the title of a selection within a publication, such as a magazine article.

Sources are not "available" unless their location is known. As the investigation proceeds, record on each card the call number or location in the library of that particular source. The location might be in the upper left hand corner, as it is in the card catalog.

The following is a sample, illustrating the details mentioned above:

051
Ou 82

       Dunlap, O. E., Jr.

       "Shall Advertising Be Given the Air?"

       Outlook, Vol. 141 (November 11, 1925),
            pp. 387-388

The bibliography of a study is the bibliography of the available sources. In collecting titles from the *Readers' Guide,* check with the periodical list of the library to be sure that the magazines are available. Note which are current, which bound and under call number in the periodical list, which unbound and in the periodical room. (Some may be in the bindery.)

Bring your cards to class and exchange with a classmate. Examine the cards you receive to consult with him on a plan for a study. Record your suggestions and criticisms as you proceed:

1. Are the cards in proper form, with the locations noted?
2. Does the bibliography seem well selected, the subject well focused, the study of reasonable magnitude?
3. Consider the titles of recent date. Are they well related and of sufficient importance? Will the study meet the assignment and be up-to-date?
4. Are there certain authors, or certain periodicals which should receive particular attention?
5. Are certain articles more general and consequently more suitable as a starting point?
6. Do subtopics suggest themselves that might fit into a future plan or outline?

Write out your suggestions and give them with the cards to your classmate. Discuss the plan with him if he wishes. When your cards are returned to you, you may wish to discuss your classmate's suggestions for your own plan.

Written Report. When you return to your room, reconsider your plan for your own study. Write your comments on your classmate's advice and hand them in to your instructor with your statement as to your decision:

1. State your subject as definitely as you can.
2. State your reasons for choosing this subject for research.
3. State what you hope to find out in reference to what your titles suggest that you can find out.
4. State how many source cards you have in all.

5. List, with full bibliographical description, the six sources that you plan to read first.

6. List additional titles that have appeared in the past year.

A Note on the Investigator's Attitude. The cause of human justice made a great stride forward when the accused was first permitted to employ an advocate. While the criminal lawyer is a shyster when he manufactures or falsifies evidence, it is nevertheless the advocate's moral duty—*even over his own convictions*—to put the case for his client in as favorable a light as possible within the bounds of truth. For circumstances may look black against an innocent man—so black that his advocate doubts his innocence, so black that he himself can be persuaded he must be guilty. And justice is more concerned with the protection of the innocent than with the punishment of the guilty. The advocate is bound to prove his case.

But that is not the way of an investigator. He is not bound to prove his case, he is bound to discover the facts about a matter. His attitude toward his hypothesis is quite different. He must not be determined to prove his case. He must look upon it merely as a picture of what might be proved—a picture to give shape and direction to his study, but a picture to be modified and changed as the findings require. He must keep an open mind.

But an open mind is not a blank mind. The investigator must speculate and try to predict the shape of things to come. The first clues will come from the titles of the selected sources. But as the reading proceeds, new points will be suggested, and new questions will arise. The investigator's plan may be modified as fresh and even contradictory evidence comes to light. But, unlike the advocate, the investigator is not disappointed to have his plan upset. The upsetting discovery may be the gateway to adventure in new ideas.

N.B. This is not the plan of a paper. It is the plan of a study. Do not approach your study with a debater's mind.

The *paper* cannot be planned until the results are ready to report.

3. The Notes for a Compilation

It would be safer, perhaps, if the writer could always have his sources at hand while he writes. Then he might need notes only as memoranda for cross reference.

But in even a brief compilation that is rarely possible. The investigator must read and take notes in the library and write the paper at home. His notes must be such that he can substitute them for the source without danger of misstatement or misquotation. He must not trust his memory after even a brief interval.

Furthermore, in a compilation, he cannot know the order of reference to his material until all the data are collected. His notes must be taken in units that can be reorganized at any time. Any given source is likely to contain material on several subtopics of the investigation. Therefore there must be as many separate notes as there are page references and subtopics. (The idea is not to have more on one note than will be used at one point in the paper.) Then, at any time, the investigator can distribute his notes, classifying them by the subtopics of his investigation, and still be able at any time to return them to the original order of continuity in the source.

The following diagram shows a possible distribution of five data cards from two sources:

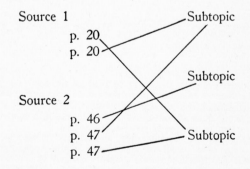

It is important that notes not be mixed up as they are handled. Bibliographical notes should be placed on 3″ × 5″ cards. Then they will not be overlooked if they are temporarily handled with the data notes. Data notes should be placed on 4″ × 6″ cards, which should be reserved only for the recording of data from reading. Other memoranda should be placed on a different stationery, except for brief bracketed comments within the data notes. (The data note itself is a *record,* not an interpretation.) Then if the investigator should forget to record the page reference on a data card, he will at least know that it is a data note and will not treat it as some observation of his own. (That is easier to do than one might suppose. One should never trust one's memory in a compilation.)

The procedure of note-taking is this.[6] With the source at hand, first check the bibliographical description on the source card. Be sure that the author's name is written as it appears in the source. Record the full page-span exactly. Then decide on a source key—a brief name or number that will distinguish the source from all others and economize the effort of note-taking. Place this key in the upper right-hand corner of the source card and repeat it in the upper right-hand corner of all the data notes taken from the source.

After the data note is taken on a 4″ × 6″ card, label it in the upper left-hand corner with a brief heading or "slug"[7] that will relate its content to the subtopic in the investigation.

These details are illustrated in the following notes from Carson's investigation:[8]

---

[6] Some students prefer at this stage to read all the material first and then, with a definite plan in mind, return to the sources to extract the data notes. This is a good method, *if you have the time.*

[7] The newspaper term is convenient here, suggesting a temporary labeling until the final place in the paper can be determined.

[8] These are copies of Carson's notes, which were written in pencil. Topliff's original notes from Buell are reproduced in the Appendix, pp. 127 ff.

621.384193   4
F 51

   Firth, Ivan Eustace, and Erskine, Gladys Shaw

   Gateway to Radio

   New York: The Macaulay Co., 1934

Popularity of A&Andy   4

                                        p. 277

   At height of popularity of Amos & Andy, telephone company reported the biggest falling off in business at the time they were on. [Shows how big an audience may be reached.]

Full value of radio   4

                                        p. 298

   "Until the sponsors and all those responsible have a greater respect for the radio audience, which can only be achieved by that audience showing a greater respect for themselves and for the programs brought into their homes, the full entertaining and cultural value of radio will not be obtained."

As the notes are taken, it must be remembered that a data note is valueless without the exact page reference to the source. The source key otherwise can be the briefest possible, as the data should always be examined with the source card at hand as a check on matters of dating, authority, etc. Each note should have a brief label or "slug," so that the investigator will not forget why he took it.

In general, the investigator should not accumulate many direct quotations. If he wants quotation, he should take it, and if any phrase seems distinctive, he should put it in quotation marks in his summary. But, in general, one should consider the information that he wants and put it down, fully and understandably, in telegraphic style. Then, when he uses the information later, he will find it ready to be phrased in his own way, in a manner appropriate to his own discussion. Quotation, on the other hand, must be recorded without the slightest alteration, even of a misprint. A misprint may be indicated thus: "dosg [dogs] and cats," or thus: "dosg [*sic*] and cats." Any inserted comment is bracketed. (If you underline a part, be sure to bracket that the italics are yours.) Parts may be omitted, provided that the omission does not distort the sense of the part retained. An omission is indicated by the mark of ellipsis (three successive dots), with a fourth dot if the omission includes the end of a sentence. Quotation marks within the quoted passage should be changed to single quotes when the quoted passage is placed within quotation marks.

Assignment B3

Bring to class the bibliographical cards and all data notes from two sources. Select at least one note from each source and combine these notes in a brief passage, documenting carefully. This differs from Assignment A in that it may be briefer —merely a passage, and in that it is to be written from the notes rather than from the source.

The purpose of this assignment is to test two things:

1. That the note is a safe substitute for the source. Never pretend to quote, directly or indirectly, from memory. There should be nothing from the source in the paper that is not clearly in the note.
2. That the note is a convenient tool of organization. It should be short—usually one or two sentences, certainly no more than one side of a 4″ × 6″ card; it should be clearly labeled and have exact page reference to the source.

Enclose all the note cards, including those not used in the passage.

N.B. It is not important that the notes be attractive. They are yours. Just be sure that they are safe, accurate, and intelligible records. There should be no attempt to make data cards away from the source.

4. The Make-up of a Formal Report

The formal report is placed flat in a cover and is made up of the following essential parts:

> Title page
> Table of contents
> Documented text
> Bibliography

All manuscript is written on one side only. If typewritten, it is double spaced; footnotes, bibliographical entries, verbatim blocks, and tabulated items are single spaced but have double space between them. Footnote symbols are raised above the line.

Assignment B4

When from a judicious selection of sources you have satisfied your curiosity, organize your data and present a report of your findings, documenting carefully. Place your unexamined sources in a supplementary bibliography for future reference and for a present check on the wisdom of your selections for the bibliography proper. Give the report a table of contents that will show your plan. Word the title carefully. Place the whole in a report cover, with all the pages face up.

Title Page. Place your title on the title page. Subtitle it, "A Research Paper." Add your by-line, the date, and whatever other details the instructor of your course requires.

Avoid what a famous scientist has called the "Error of the Improper Title." The "proper" title contains as many words as are required to indicate the exact nature of the contents.[9] Study Carson's title with reference to the content of his report.

Table of Contents. The table of contents furnishes a guide to the reading of your paper. It presents your main divisions and their subdivisions in logical series in the order they come in your paper, with page reference to where the division begins. The outline form is generally acceptable. Keep the outline parts proportionate in length to the divisions of the discussion. Avoid long series and single subpoints. Within a series, keep the wording of the coordinates in parallel structure.

Documented Text. Perhaps unfortunately, there is no one standard for the conventions of documentation and bibliographical entry. The inconsistencies in some fields are the librarian's despair.

But that does not mean that the writer can be careless about conventions. In all conventional matters one should be in style, and should be *consistent* in following it. Styles vary and change, as in matters of dress and contract bridge. But one cannot be a good bridge player without a consistent convention. So it is with documentation. The Carson paper illustrates a widely accepted convention. It also represents the maximum economy generally advisable in a formal report. The Blythe and Gongwer papers (pp. 7-8, 43-50) illustrate accepted economies for less formal writing. Consider the purpose of your reference in your own report; decide upon your appropriate convention; and use it consistently and intelligently. Use a consistent system and style of numbering, indenting, abbreviating, punctuating. Suit your documentation to your reader's needs.

---

[9] This point is taken from chap. x (p. 128) of *The Way of an Investigator,* by Walter Bradford Cannon (New York: W. W. Norton & Co., Inc., 1945). This autobiography of a famous physiologist is a good book for any investigator to read.

Everything that contributes to the discussion should be placed in the wording of the paragraph, and the discussion should be clear without reference to the footnotes. The footnotes are strong parentheses carrying details of reference for the reader, should he require them.

When several sources are used in the same paper, care must be taken to prevent any confusion of the references. The footnotes should read independently and in clear sequence:

1. When several sources are used in the same paper, the first footnote to any source should carry the full description, even though part has been given in the paragraph above.[10] Thus the footnotes are independent of the text.

2. When the footnote refers to the same source as the *immediately preceding* footnote, the abbreviation *ibid.* (*ibidem* is Latin for "in the same place") is used, followed by the page reference, if it is different. Where the paper, like Blythe's, is a commentary on a single source, *ibid.* is superfluous; otherwise it should be used. Many other Latin abbreviations have been in use in footnoting. If you run across them in reading, you can find their meaning in the dictionary. You will probably not be required to use them in writing, as the present trend is toward simplification and economy.

3. When the footnote refers to the same source as a previous footnote not immediately preceding, the author's name or a condensed title is sufficient, followed by the page reference, even when it is the same. (See Carson's footnotes 5, 19, and 20; [11] Gongwer's, 6, 7, and 9.[12]) The incomplete description tells the reader to look elsewhere in the paper for the full description. Care must be taken that the short form does not describe two previously mentioned sources. If there are two works by the same author, the title must be added.

---

[10] When a single source is used, Blythe's is a good economy, p. 7. Compare this with Ryan's, p. 9.

[11] Pp. 71, 79.

[12] P. 47.

4. It is generally preferable to keep the footnote sequence independent of the bibliography, as in Carson's paper. Gongwer's practice, however, of using short forms throughout the footnotes is coming into increasingly wider acceptance, particularly for less formal papers not intended for publication.[13]

In the convention followed by Carson, the footnotes generally read as they would in a paper without a bibliography. The exception is that when a book is described in the appended bibliography the footnote need not mention place, publisher, and date. When mentioned in a footnote, these are included parenthetically, when followed by page reference.[14] (In the bibliography they have no parenthesis.)

Above the footnotes, in typescript or manuscript, a line must be drawn from the left-hand margin to indicate the turning of the page of the text. When making your copy, keep in mind that every footnote symbol robs your page of approximately three spaces. Allow for this.

A final word as to the form of the report: In your introduction, make clear what you intend to report. In the body of the paper, maintain a firm continuity that will keep your outline before the reader; keep the connection clear in the wording; write in the interpretation of your data. In your conclusion, round out your report so that the reader will feel that his expectancy has been fulfilled. Study the Carson report as a model for the exposition.

Bibliography. The bibliography of a research paper tabulates in alphabetical order all *documentary* sources referred to in the study, whether or not they appear in the footnotes. If the bibliography is long, it may be subdivided, alphabetizing separately works of general reference, books, periodical articles, etc. Carson's bibliography[15] shows such subdivision.

---

[13] See pp. 45 ff.
[14] See footnote, p. 11.
[15] P. 80.

The main bibliography lists the sources actually read for the study. The discriminating writer may prefer to distinguish the sources actually referred to in the discussion. Noll does this.[16]

If there are additional relevant works which were not referred to, it is advisable to list these in a "supplementary bibliography." This follows the same form as the bibliography proper and reflects your acquaintance with the titles of sources not read. Perhaps time did not permit the reading of all of them; or you felt they were of lesser importance than those which you did read; or perhaps they were temporarily unavailable at the time of your study—in the bindery, out on loan, mislaid, or lost. By listing them, you forestall the criticism of being ignorant of them. Yet, since you have made no use of them, they do not belong in your bibliography proper. Topliff's paper [17] shows this practice well. Carson's paper represents a completed study.

The bibliography gives the full page span referred to in the *study,* whereas the footnotes give the exact page or pages referred to at points of the *discussion.* The footnote is a kind of parenthesis in the sentence structure of the text, and is punctuated and constructed accordingly. The bibliography, on the other hand, is a table, and each individual entry is a unit. The author's surname is placed first, and the tabular indenting of the line creates a pointing finger indicating the place in the alphabetical order of the bibliography as a whole. A period separates the author and the other main parts of the description. The place, publisher, and date of a book are given without parenthesis. A close study of the Carson paper and the illustrations of Assignment B will reveal these differences.

Written Report. With your report, submit your notes to your instructor for an additional check upon your procedure: your data notes in the order of your footnotes, your source cards divided and alphabetized as they appear in your bibliography.

---

[16] P. 41.
[17] P. 109.

Illustrations of Assignment B

News in an Old Subject. The writers of the illustrations in this section used the Carson paper as a model and followed the procedures described in the preceding assignments. When Noll went to the *Readers' Guide* to discover a subject, he was interested to find the coat-of-arms a current topic. Out of this grew his curiosity to relate the present emphasis to the earlier history of heraldry. The following paper is the result. This is a particularly good illustration of the assignment in that it shows the expansion of the bibliography from the current articles to older books and magazines.

Students frequently like to illustrate their papers. Good illustrations add to the attractiveness of a paper, and a well-placed map or diagram will often clear up a point not easily expressed in words alone. The student who wishes to illustrate his paper is advised to consult illustrated publications to discover the various methods. It is important that illustrative material be placed where it will be most useful to the reader.

Noll has listed his Illustration Sheet in his table of contents. Where a paper has a number of maps or figures, they are often given a separate table, following the table of contents.

HERALDRY, ANCIENT AND MODERN

A Research Paper

by

Philip C. Noll

English 31-M
Miss Johnson
December 30, 1949
Theme 12 (Outside)
Noll, Philip C.

Table of Contents

HERALDRY, ANCIENT AND MODERN

Heraldry is an ancient science. It began in times before the Crusades and extends to the present. Since customs change through the centuries, there must have been various phases of heraldry as time progressed. In order to show how the science developed, an over-all picture will be given touching on the earliest known instances, some high spots as time went on, and present usages. Then a detailed account will be given showing how heraldry is a science. To fill out the picture, some facts are included about London's College of Arms, and an illustration sheet is attached to explain certain figures which are difficult to describe in writing.

When the word "heraldry" is mentioned, most people immediately think of the family coat-of-arms. But when they stop to consider the word, they realize that it must mean more than facts concerning family emblems. Indeed, the early English herald had many jobs. Among other such duties, he was his master's messenger, he was chief recorder of chivalrous deeds in his household, he was in charge of tournaments, and he was keeper of all his master's records and matters pertaining to genealogy and precedence.[1] For this reason, probably, the word heraldry meant everything associated with royalty, shining armor, and gleaming bright colors. But the word as used today applies to only one of these many concerns, that of armorial bearings, or coats-of-arms.

The first use of designs to represent a person or family came long before the English herald. One historian jokingly said, "Adam bore a red shield upon which the arms of Eve, a shield of argent, were

---

[1] C. Maynard and M. L. Keech, "The Science of Heraldry," *Hobbies*, Vol. 54 (September, 1949), p. 159.

2

quartered as an escutcheon of pretense, she being an heiress .... the emblazonry was probably carried on their fig leaves." [2] Seriously, though, ancient warriors used, as their only defense weapon, the shield. From woven wicker and willow-wood slabs, the shield gradually evolved to metal. The warriors painted designs on their shields to identify themselves to friends and to frighten their foes. Later, Benvenuto Cellini or Antonio Pollaiuolo made these designs works of art.[3] Sometimes these designs were painted on the warrior's coat instead of on his shield—thus the term coat-of-arms.[4] Gradually, the idea of having a particular design or coat-of-arms for each family spread throughout Europe, and by the end of the tenth century, coats-of-arms appeared which were used solely to represent a family or clan.[5] It was probably in the twelfth or thirteenth century that the English herald appeared. Many tournaments were held in England during and after the Crusades, and the winner of each tournament was awarded badges and other decorations to be affixed to his armor and shield. At some period in the thirteenth century, the awarding of these badges became an organized procedure subject to fixed rules.[6]

The profound importance that a simple design can have in public

---

[2] D. R. Barton, "The Story of Heraldry," Natural History, Vol. 45 (March, 1940) , p. 185.

[3] L. D. Gardel, "Badges of Nobility," Américas, Vol. 1 (June, 1949) , p. 29.

[4] F. J. Grant, Lord Lyon King of Arms, The Manual of Heraldry, p. 1.

[5] Gardel, p. 29.

[6] C. A. Bennett, "High School Heraldry," Industrial Education Magazine, Vol. 38 (November, 1936), p. 230.

thought and action showed itself in England in the fifteenth century. In the War of the Roses, many noblemen were killed and they left unclaimed estates. By this time, the King had established a royal Herald's Office, and people came in droves to this office to check on their family genealogy and coat-of-arms. Their one purpose, of course, was to establish themselves as rightful heirs to all the unclaimed land. During this period, heraldry suffered a setback. Using counterfeit or faked coats-of-arms, many people were granted illegal ownership of estates.[7]

The new socialist party in Great Britain has given rise to more work for the Herald's Office. Many coal, electric, and other public utilities have recently been nationalized by Prime Minister Attlee's system. This means that their position has been raised so that they can now apply for their own armorial insignia.[8]

Steamships of many countries have shed their wartime grey and they now show brilliant markings on their funnels. The designs are not like the familiar English coat-of-arms, but they signify practically the same things. Some designs tell the ship's home country, the steamship line, and perhaps some interesting history about the ship. Each American ship has her markings registered with the Commissioner of Customs, Treasury Department, Washington, D.C., to prevent duplication.[9] Airplanes, too, bear their owners' coats-of-arms. Cap-

---

[7] Barton, p. 186.

[8] Benjamin Welles, "Heraldry Rampant, London's College of Arms," New York Times Magazine, April 10, 1949, p. 64.

[9] Lucy Greenbaum, "Heraldry of the Sea," New York Times Magazine, January 13, 1946, p. 47.

4

tain Eddie Rickenbacker in World War I had a mark on his plane to distinguish him from the rest. It was a disc with a glossy ringmaster's high silk hat which signified his leadership of the famed flying circus.[10]

Designers of military insignia use practices of heraldry in their work. The location of a regiment's home base, where and when the regiment was formed, and some of its major victories are sometimes shown on its insignia.[11]

Since the countries in the British Isles have the most extensive records and rules regarding heraldry, a study of it in these countries alone will yield much information. The facts and rules given here will concern English heraldry alone unless otherwise stated.

In studies which are sciences, we are concerned with the definition of the word science. Here, we will take "science" to mean coordinated and systematized knowledge of some subject or group of allied subjects. At the end of this discussion, we will see that heraldry is truly a science.

A coat-of-arms can consist of many parts. Some arms are very elaborate while others seem too simple. The best description of a coat-of-arms would give only the more important parts. A fair description follows. A coat-of-arms consists of four principal parts: the shield, in the center; the crest, which is the design directly above the shield (usually some sort of headgear or a wreath) ; the supporters (background), usually figures of animals or people holding the shield; and the motto, usually on a scroll at the very top or bottom of the

---

[10] Barton, p. 187.

[11] "Heraldic Designs Form Army's Regimental Insignia," Popular Science, June, 1941, p. 64.

5

coat-of-arms. The shield is the most important part.[12] As an incidental note about backgrounds or supporters, the Herald's College,
in keeping with the times, has been using tractors, coal mines, and gas
reservoirs as supporters on recently granted arms. The shield can be
in any shape but is usually a normal shield. There is one exception
in that unmarried women who have their own coats-of-arms have a
diamond-shaped lozenge instead of a shield.[13] (See Illustration Sheet,
page 9.)

It was mentioned in the description of a coat-of-arms that the
shield is the most important part. Almost all of the information and
history which is on a coat-of-arms is on the shield. Any design on the
shield is called a charge, and the shield can be "charged" with almost
any form of human, animal, bird, or geometrical design or combination
of these.[14] The top of the shield is the chief, and the bottom is the
base. To a bearer of the shield, the right side of it is the dexter
side, and the left is the sinister side. The midpoint of the shield is
called the fess point.[15]

The more common of the geometrical designs on the shield are
called ordinaries, and the less common, subordinaries. Writers on
heraldry seem to disagree as to which are ordinaries and which are
subordinaries. The list of ordinaries given here seems to agree with
the majority of the sources studied. The ordinaries are the bend, bend

---

[12] M. M. Hutcheson, "Animals and Flowers Important in Crests
and Emblems," Nature Magazine, May, 1939, p. 252.

[13] Welles, p. 64.

[14] Ibid.

[15] Grant, p. 17.

sinister, chevron, chief, cross, fess, pale, pile, saltire (see Illustration
Sheet). These are simple designs and may originally have been metal
bands used to strengthen the shield. Each design has its own meaning,
but the meanings were adopted long after the designs were first used.[16]

Probably the thing which makes coats-of-arms so attractive is their
bright color. Overall color patterns are divided into three groups.
These are colors, metals, and furs. A. C. Fox-Davies in his book
Heraldry lists the colors and metals adequately. The metals are hues,
just like the colors, but they are called metals because they represent
gold and silver. They are called "or" and "argent" respectively.
The colors are red, "gules"; blue, "azure"; green, "vert"; purple,
"purpure"; and black, "sable." There are a few others but these are
most common.[17] The third color pattern is the furs. These might
have originated in primitive times when savages decorated their shields
with animal skins. They are explained better in another source. As
used today, furs are only color patterns used on coats-of-arms, and
not actual skins. The fur "ermine" is black designs representing
ermine skins on a white background. "Ermines" is just the reverse
of this, white designs on a black background. "Erminois" is gold
designs on black, while "pean" is black on gold. The fur "vair" does
not look like the ermine group. It is alternately blue and silver.[18]
See Illustration Sheet for an example of "vair."

Since there are so many ways in which the shield may be decorated,
just one interesting example will be given here as an illustration. A

----

[16] Maynard and Keech, p. 158.

[17] A. C. Fox-Davies, A Complete Guide to Heraldry, p. 67.

[18] Maynard and Keech, p. 158.

certain Lord Augustus Fitzroy was the illegitimate grandson of King Charles II of England. So according to heraldic practices, Fitzroy's coat-of-arms was the same as that of King Charles, except that a "baton sinister" (see Illustration Sheet) was affixed across its face. A "baton sinister" (sometimes called bar sinister) in heraldry is used to denote illegitimacy. When Fitzroy married one Elizabeth Cosby, the two united their coats-of-arms side by side on one shield, thus making an original coat-of-arms for that family. Such a uniting on one shield is called "impaling." After Fitzroy's death, the widow Elizabeth had their coat-of-arms painted on a dinner service, but with the baton sinister omitted, probably to avert gossip. This left the arms of King Charles on one half of the shield, and Elizabeth's arms on the other, and thus told the miraculous story that she had married King Charles himself! [19]

For the description of a shield there are many other technical terms and procedures used which are too numerous to discuss here. Some practices used in describing the shield are shown on the Illustration Sheet.

London's College of Arms was founded by King Richard III in 1484, and the College has family records dating back to the fifteenth century. The officers of the College are installed for life and each must have a working knowledge of genealogy, history, languages, law, and draftsmanship. Each officer must have a private income, since the pay from the crown is only £49 (about $196) per year (as of April 10, 1949). The College's job consists in granting new coats-of-arms

---

[19] A. Tudor-Craig, "In Pursuit of a Pedigree," Saturday Evening Post, March 21, 1936, p. 25.

8

and answering some 500-odd requests per week for heraldic information.[20]

The Herald's College is under the supervision of the Earl Marshall. The officers of the College consist of three Kings, named after the Orders of Knighthood Garter, Clarenceaux, and Norroy; six Heralds, named after the cities Chester, Lancaster, Richmond, Somerset, Windsor, and York; and four Pursuivants, named Rouge Croix, Blue Mantle, Roughe Dragon, and Portcullis.[21]

---

[20] Welles, pp. 63f.

[21] Maynard and Keech, p. 159.

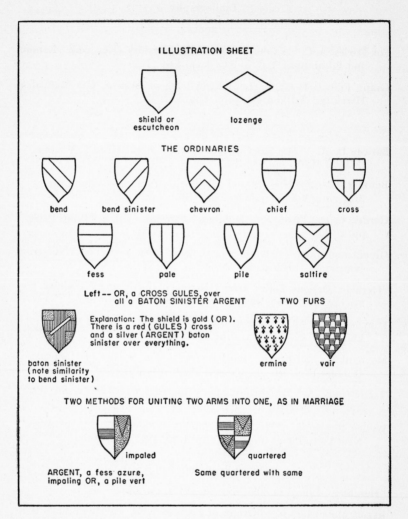

ILLUSTRATION SHEET

shield or escutcheon   lozenge

THE ORDINARIES

bend   bend sinister   chevron   chief   cross

fess   pale   pile   saltire

Left-- OR, a CROSS GULES, over
all a BATON SINISTER ARGENT   TWO FURS

Explanation: The shield is gold (OR).
There is a red (GULES) cross
and a silver (ARGENT) baton
sinister over everything.

baton sinister
(note similarity
to bend sinister)   ermine   vair

TWO METHODS FOR UNITING TWO ARMS INTO ONE, AS IN MARRIAGE

impaled   quartered

ARGENT, a fess azure,
impaling OR, a pile vert   Same quartered with same

Adapted from Francis J. W. S. Grant, The Manual of Heraldry, passim.

10

Bibliography

Books

Fox-Davies, A. C. A Complete Guide to Heraldry (Rev. ed.). London and Edinburgh: T.C. & E.C. Jack, Ltd., 1929.

Grant, Francis J. W. S. (Lord Lyon King of Arms). The Manual of Heraldry. Edinburgh: John Grant, 1929.

Articles

Barton, D. R. "The Story of Heraldry," Natural History, Vol. 45 (March, 1940), pp. 184-187.

Bennett, C. A. "High School Heraldry," Industrial Education Magazine, Vol. 38 (November, 1936), pp. 230-234.

Gardel, L. D. "Badges of Nobility," Américas, Vol. 1 (June, 1949), pp. 29-30.

Greenbaum, Lucy. "Heraldry of the Sea," New York Times Magazine, January 13, 1946, p. 47.

"Heraldic Designs Form Army's Regimental Insignia," Popular Science, Vol. 138 (June, 1941), pp. 64-65.

Hutcheson, M. M. "Animals and Flowers Important in Crests and Emblems," Nature Magazine, Vol. 32 (May, 1939), pp. 252-255.

Maynard, C., and Keech, Mabel Louise. "The Science of Heraldry," Hobbies, Vol. 54 (September, 1949), pp. 157-159.

Tudor-Craig, A. "In Pursuit of a Pedigree," Saturday Evening Post, Vol. 208 (March 21, 1936), pp. 24-25.

Welles, Benjamin. "Heraldry Rampant, London's College of Arms," New York Times Magazine, April 10, 1949, pp. 63-64.

Articles Read but Not Used

"Heraldry," Life, Vol. 22 (May 26, 1947), pp. 68-69.

Keech, Mabel Louise. "Origin of Coats-of-Arms, to Whom They Were Granted, and Usages," Hobbies, Vol. 46 (June, 1941), pp. 117-118.

Shaw, J. "Arms of Glasgow," Hobbies, Vol. 53 (December, 1948), p. 50.

11

Supplementary Bibliography

Pedrick, Gale.   A Manual of Heraldry.   Philadelphia: J. B. Lippincott
Co., n.d.

Wilson, P. W.   "Churchill in Heraldry," New York Times Magazine,
September 26, 1943, p. 20.

Report of a Brief Study. The following report does not pretend to represent a complete study. The writer wished to satisfy his curiosity on certain points, with reference to the problem in his home community.

Note that in works like encyclopedias, where articles appear in alphabetical order, the reader rarely needs the number to find the page. Note also that for works so widely known the full facts of publication rarely need to be supplied, even in the bibliography.

As mentioned previously, Gongwer's footnote economies are coming into use for less formal papers. Since the sources are described in the bibliography, short forms are used throughout the footnotes. Yet the paper is, for its purposes, adequately documented. In formal writing, Carson's practice is still preferable.

SCHOOL CONSOLIDATION

A Research Paper

by

Ralph A. Gongwer

English 31-AJ
Miss Johnson
June 2, 1949
Research theme

Table of Contents

SCHOOL CONSOLIDATION

I

The movement toward the consolidation of schools began in New York State in 1853, when an act was passed by the State Legislature permitting consolidation. This act was known as the Union School Law, incorporated as Title IX of the Consolidated Act of 1864.[1] However, New York was not the first state to take advantage of a school consolidation act. Massachusetts quickly considered the advantages and established the first consolidated school in Concord in 1869. At first the school included only two of the old districts, but before ten years had elapsed, every district in the city had been abolished by a popular vote, and the school was the educational center for the entire city.[2]

After it was found that consolidation solved many of the educational problems confronting the people, the movement spread rapidly. Excellent progress has been made in consolidation in the North Central States.[3] In 1930 consolidated schools were increasing at the rate of about one thousand a year, and the number of one-teacher schools was gradually diminishing. In 1929 there were approximately 16,500 consolidated schools in the United States with 160,000 teachers and 3,200,000 pupils.[4] Figuring the rate at one thousand a year and the number of consolidated schools in 1929 as 16,500, there should

[1] "Consolidation of Schools," Encyclopedia Americana.

[2] "School," World Book Encyclopedia, Vol. 15, p. 6423.

[3] "Consolidation of Schools."

[4] "School," p. 6424.

be 36,500 consolidated schools in the present year, 1949. However, this large number should not fool anyone. It is calculated on the basis of schools all over the country; consequently, it takes into consideration all of the one-room school houses in the South and in the mountain area in the West. Very few districts with an enrollment of more than two hundred students have been consolidated. There is one case in Lagro Township, Indiana, where there are three different schools. One has an enrollment of three hundred while the other two have only one hundred students each. These three schools are less than ten miles apart!

II

No matter what kind of project one may try to establish and maintain, he will always encounter some factors which influence his decisions. This is true in school building as well as in private business. Although school enrollments, shifting school populations, reorganization, fires, and obsolescence of school buildings all influence building construction to a great extent, high labor and material costs seem to be the big stumbling block in consolidation.[5]

School building costs are high at the present time and everyone knows it. According to one building index, the average cost of labor and materials for school buildings stands at 185 per cent of the corresponding 1939 price level. Still another report, the National Index, states that construction costs are now more than 200 per cent of prewar costs. However, in neither case do these indexes allow for the cushion

---

[5] John J. Krill, "A Big Job in 1949," p. 17.

3

in contractors' bids which protects them against loss in the event of further increase in cost of materials and labor. Some of these cushions are as high as 25 per cent of the construction cost.[6] Even with the tremendous cost figure facing them, many districts are finding it wise to go ahead and build. A few school districts have been able to save some money in the last few years, but the bulk of them have to finance their buildings in one of two ways or by the combination of the two ways.

The first method and the one that is most often used is the "pay as you use" method. This method calls for a direct current tax levy and a bond issue.[7] The "pay as you use" method has been found to be very satisfactory to both the parents of the students and the rest of the taxpayers in the district. This method was used to finance the Lake View Junior-Senior High School in Indiana. The building contains 1,030,000 cubic feet and the cost for labor, materials, and furnishings was about $624,000. The district was able to construct at this price by having the building built under three contracts.[8]

The other method is the "pay as you build" method.[9] In this case a school tax increase must be levied for several years in order to accumulate the money before the building is constructed. This is a much slower method than the one previously mentioned, but the two can be combined into a very satisfactory arrangement.

------

[6] I. A. Booker, "Build That School House Now," p. 31.

[7] Ibid.

[8] H. B. Green, B. B. Burgess, and L. V. Dewitt, "Senior-Junior High," p. 45.

[9] Booker, p. 31.

4

In the consolidation of several schools in Robertson County, Indiana, the Board of Education recommended the merger plan to the County Court. The plan was to call for $2,000,000. $1,600,000 was to be raised through the sale of bonds and the remainder, or $400,000, was to be raised by a general sales tax levied over a period of five years.[10]

III

Before action can be started on the consolidation of schools in a district, certain information must be gathered and considered. The first job is to get accurate information on the building needs of the district. If the district is going to have a large increase or decrease in population, if the district should have two large schools instead of one, if the district needs better transportation facilities—all of these things must be considered. The next step is to plan a clear and convincing program to present intelligently to the people. The third step is to develop a preliminary plan which can be consistent with educational services.[11] The fourth and last step is to consider the cost of the project and whether the district can afford this price.

In one district small committees were organized in each community to survey the needs and possibilities. These committees then brought the whole community together in a series of mass meetings. Experts gave talks on the advantages of consolidation in the particular district, and then the county had a rally at the county seat. Here

---

[10] Gene H. Sloan, "Robertson County Schools Consolidate," p. 23.
[11] Booker, p. 31.

5

the County Court, leaders of the community, and others who had
helped presented more advantages of the new program.[12] Considering
all these facts, one can safely say that if a consolidation of schools
is needed, the first job is to get the taxpayers of the district interested
in a consolidated school.

---

[12] Sloan, p. 24.

6

Bibliography

Booker, I. A.   "Build That School House Now," National Education Association Journal, Vol. 38 (Jan. 1949), pp. 30-1.

"Consolidation of Schools," Encyclopedia Americana, Vol. 7 (1946).

Green, H. B., Burgess, B. B., and DeWitt, L. V.   "Senior-Junior High," Nation's Schools, Vol. 43 (Apr. 1949), pp. 44-5.

Krill, John J.   "A Big Job in 1949," American School Board Journal, Vol. 118 (Jan. 1949), p. 17.

"School," World Book Encyclopedia, Vol. 15 (1941), pp. 6423-4.

Sloan, Gene H.   "Robertson County Schools Consolidate," American School Board Journal, Vol. 118 (Jan. 1949), pp. 21-4.

Supplementary Bibliography

Brodinsky, B. P.   "Farmer's Hopes about Schools," Nation's Schools, Vol. 43 (Feb. 1949), pp. 28-32.

Cocking, W. D.   "School, a Center of Community Living," American City, Vol. 63 (Dec. 1948), p. 119.

Meyer, A. E.   "Are Our Public Schools Doing Their Job?" Atlantic Monthly, Vol. 183 (Feb. 1949), pp. 32-6.

Oliver, A. J.   "How Big Should the Small School Be?" School and Society, Vol. 69 (Feb. 1949), pp. 127-8.

Perkins, L. H.   "Rural Consolidated," Nation's Schools, Vol. 43 (Feb. 1949), pp. 40-3.

Ragsdale, C. E.   "New High School for Rural Youth, Wisconsin," Education for Victory, Vol. 3 (May 3, 1945), pp. 5-7.

Smart, C. H., and Holden, E. B.   "Consolidated School," Nation's Schools, Vol. 43 (Apr. 1949), pp. 41-4.

Stinnett, T. M.   "Maybe They Won't Believe It, but It's True!" National Education Association Journal, Vol. 38 (Jan. 1949), pp. 27-8.

Historical Research in Engineering. Engineers are in the majority in composition classes at Purdue. Their minority representation in this text is explained by the fact that the engineer has less professional need for historical research. Engineering reports generally present data derived from other sources than literature. Here, however, an engineer has found private use for the techniques in bringing himself up to date on a development in his field.

Notice the documentation economies in this paper. The reader of an article frequently likes to glance at the footnotes to check such matters as dating and authority. He has no immediate need for the volume numbers, and these need not clutter the footnotes when they are supplied in the appended bibliography.

The experienced writer generally uses greater economy than is shown in the bibliography of this paper. In publication, particularly, "Vol." and "p." are ordinarily omitted when both numbers are given, and the volume number usually appears as a Roman numeral. Since it is so easy to make errors, however, the novice is advised to label his numbers and not attempt to translate to Roman numerals. Economy is a matter of convenience and saving. The important thing is intelligibility and accuracy.

NEW DEVELOPMENTS IN HOME HEATING

A Research Paper

by

Lloyd E. Grove

English 31-F
Miss Johnson
August 13, 1949
No. 14 (Outside)
Grove, Lloyd E.

Table of Contents

NEW DEVELOPMENTS IN HOME HEATING

The operation of a heating system is one of the greatest expenses incurred by a home owner; and as if this expense were not high enough, authorities agree that fuel costs will increase even further because fuel resources are rapidly being used up. In view of this situation, some means of reducing the expense of home heating and the rate of fuel consumption should be put in use.

Insulation is one of the simplest and most effective means of making any type of heating system more efficient. Complete insulation can reduce fuel requirements as much as 50 per cent; yet only one house in twenty-five is insulated.[1]

In 1948, several new types of furnaces which use fuel economically were developed. Of particular importance are the Anthratube, a coal-burning stoker and boiler; a gas-burning air conditioner manufactured by the Servel Company; and the Jet-Heet, an oil-burning furnace. All three of these attain previously unheard-of efficiencies of operation and only the Servel air conditioner is more expensive than the average furnace now in use.[2]

Even though these systems show improved efficiencies, the fact remains that fuel prices are steadily increasing and that shortages may occur when heat is needed most. Their use still requires a sizeable percentage of the country's fuel resources. From the conservationist's

------

[1] "How to Heat a House," Fortune, September, 1948, p. 109.

[2] "What's New in House Heating?" Fortune, September, 1948, p. 145.

2

point of view, a better plan would be to search elsewhere for energy with which to heat homes.[3]

During the past two years, remarkable progress has been made toward perfecting completely new methods of home heating. Of the several advancements, the heat pump appears most promising.

The heat pump is very aptly named, since it is a device for pumping heat from one place to another. The idea is not new, since the electric refrigerator operates on the same principle; but only recently has this idea been developed enough to allow the heating of an entire house. The process may also be reversed to provide air conditioning in the summer.

According to two heating experts, Philip Sporn and E. R. Ambrose, an electrically operated heat pump can supply automatically heating, cooling, humidifying, dehumidifying, and filtering the year around. All this is accomplished with no products of combustion, no odors, no soot, no chimney, no flame, and with the use of only one utility service.[4] To make these qualities even more desirable, Wayne Snowden states, "a pound of fuel, when burned in a power station to produce electricity to run a heat pump in a home, can make the house warmer than had the pound of fuel been burned right there in the most efficient home furnace."[5]

The heat pump burns no fuel in the sense that a furnace burns

---

[3] "How to Heat a House," p. 109.

[4] Philip Sporn and E. R. Ambrose, "Heat Pump Undergoing Tests in Five Houses," Architectural Record, May, 1949, p. 142.

[5] Wayne Snowden, "Heat Without Fuel," Saturday Evening Post, September 18, 1948, p. 28.

coal; therefore, energy must be obtained from some other source. In tests made upon five houses in various parts of the country, heat from ground water, the earth itself, and the air was found to be practical for use with the heat pump; however, when the question arises as to which source is the best to use, the answer is somewhat difficult to give. Water is not always available in every location; and when available, it may require special treatment to make it chemically suitable for the purpose. The earth is a good source of constant temperature heat, but the cost of burying 120 to 450 feet of pipe beneath the frost line may be enormous. The air is always available and is the best source when low outdoor temperatures are infrequent and of short duration.[6]

In view of the fact that no one source will satisfy all needs, the best plan would be to use a combination of more than one. For example, use air when the temperature is above thirty degrees and use earth or water when it is colder.[7]

The first cost of the heat pump is rather high when compared with the cost of a conventional system. Mr. Snowden estimates that a heat pump for a small, well insulated house located where winters are not too severe would cost over two thousand dollars excluding the installation costs; whereas a conventional heating and air conditioning system would cost only sixteen hundred dollars installed.[8] These figures show why the heat pump is not on a competitive basis with the furnace at present.

------

[6] Sporn and Ambrose, p. 142.

[7] Ibid.

[8] Snowden, p. 156.

4

With the satisfactory development of the heat pump, new questions are being raised by heating engineers. Can heat removed from a refrigerator be piped to a warming oven in the kitchen? Can heat removed from packing houses, cold storage plants, and the like be used to warm offices? At the present rate of development, these questions may be answered in the very near future.[9]

Hartley E. Howe, an engineer, has stated, "The energy released by the atomic bomb is matched every day by the sunlight that falls on one-and-a-half square miles of land."[10] This realization has led to much research on the development of a home-heating plant powered by the sun.

The Solar Energy Research Department of M.I.T. has done much toward proving that solar heating can be practical. In the fall of 1948 the first solar heating system was installed in a house near Boston, Massachusetts. This system uses water circulating through a heat collector on the roof as a storage medium. A twelve-hundred-gallon tank in the attic stores the heated water until its heat is needed. The heat collector is four-hundred square feet in area and consists of a blackened sheet of metal behind two sheets of glass. Heat from the sun is absorbed by the metal and is carried to the storage tank by the water.[11]

Almost simultaneously with the project in Boston another house

---

[9] "Heating Device Uses Heat from the Ground," Business Week, April 10, 1948, p. 64.

[10] Hartley E. Howe, "Sun Furnace in Your Attic," Popular Science Monthly, March, 1949, p. 112.

[11] "M.I.T. Builds Solar-heated House," Architectural Record, April, 1949, p. 135.

5

using solar heat was built at Dover, Massachusetts, under the direction of Dr. Maria Telkes of M. I. T. In this house, heat is transferred from the collector by forced-air draft to storage bins filled with an inexpensive sodium compound capable of storing seven times as much heat as an equal weight of water. A family living in this house reported complete comfort during the entire winter.[12]

At this writing, neither of these systems has proved completely satisfactory for the average home owner. Although the principle is quite practical, the cost is rather high at present. Dr. Telkes' unit, being the more feasible to install, costs approximately three thousand dollars, and the house itself is very expensively insulated. Another factor to be considered is that Boston is about the northern limit for practical solar heating, according to Mr. Howe. Further north, the heat collector becomes too large for the house.[13] However, the future of solar heating is not dark. An engineer of the Gulf Oil Company, Eugene Ayers, states that the Telkes method can reduce the national fuel bill ten per cent in ten years.[14]

Thus far, the discussion has been centered about the source of heat. Now the problem arises concerning the method of distribution which should be used.

At present, most homes are heated by warm-air registers, steam radiators, or space heaters,—all of which provide heat by convection currents that circulate through the air. Owing to the fact that warm

---

[12] "World's First Sun-heated Home in Dover, Massachusetts," Life, May 2, 1949, p. 90.

[13] Howe, p. 108.

[14] "World's First Sun-heated Home in Dover, Massachusetts," p. 93.

6

air rises, there is a large temperature difference between the floor and the ceiling. In the case of the space heater this difference is as much as forty degrees. The steam radiator is the best convector, since the temperature difference is only fourteen degrees from floor to ceiling; however, even this figure may be improved by the use of radiant heating.[15]

Any structural surface of a room may be made a radiant panel by placing behind the surface the hot water pipes or warm air ducts which carry the heat from the source. However, the ceiling panel is in more favor because it can be operated about twenty degrees hotter than the floor or a wall panel, and there are no rugs or furniture to interfere with good radiation.[16]

Radiant heating provides warmth by means of infrared waves emitted from the panel. Since air is a poor absorber of infrared waves, nearly all available heat is used to warm the room itself and its occupants rather than the air. This allows a more uniform temperature throughout the room. In fact, the temperature difference from floor to ceiling proves to be only seven degrees when a ceiling panel is used as the radiant surface.[17]

In conclusion, I feel free to say that the new home-heating devices which are now being developed will allow the home owner to have more efficient, healthful, and economical heat in his home in the very near future.

---

[15] "How to Heat a House," p. 110.

[16] Ibid., p. 111.

[17] Ibid., p. 110.

7

Bibliography

"Fireless Furnace," Life, Vol. 25, No. 17 (October 25, 1948), pp. 83-84.

"Floor Level Heating," Architectural Record, Vol. 105, No. 4 (April, 1949), pp. 186, 188.

"Heating Device Uses Heat from the Ground," Business Week, No. 971 (April 10, 1948), pp. 63-64.

"How to Heat a House," Fortune, Vol. 38, No. 3 (September, 1948), pp. 108-113.

Howe, Hartley E.   "Sun Furnace in Your Attic," Popular Science Monthly, Vol. 154, No. 3 (March, 1949), pp. 106-112.

"M.I.T. Builds Solar-heated House," Architectural Record, Vol. 105, No. 4 (April, 1949), pp. 135-138.

Snowden, Wayne. "Heat Without Fuel," Saturday Evening Post, Vol. 221, No. 12 (September 18, 1948), pp. 28, 155-156, 158.

Sporn, Philip, and Ambrose, E. R.   "Heat Pump Undergoing Tests in Five Houses," Architectural Record, Vol. 105, No. 5 (May, 1949), pp. 140-144, 182, 184.

Strock, Clifford. "Progress in House Heating Equipment," Architectural Record, Vol. 105, No. 4 (April, 1949), pp. 139-145.

"What's New in House Heating?" Fortune, Vol. 38, No. 3 (September, 1948), p. 145.

"World's First Sun-heated Home in Dover, Massachusetts," Life, Vol. 26, No. 18 (May 2, 1949), pp. 90, 93.

Supplementary Bibliography

"How Good is Panel Heating?" Better Homes and Gardens, Vol. 27 (April, 1949), p. 268.

"Pipe for Radiant Heating: Radiant Baseboard," Architectural Record, Vol. 105 (May, 1949), p. 188.

"Warm Wall Heat," Science Illustrated, Vol. 4 (June, 1949), pp. 72-75.

II
MODELS AND ADAPTATIONS

INTRODUCTION

The preceding assignments have introduced the principal techniques of documentary research. In future papers you will adapt these techniques, combining them to serve your purpose. Many documented papers, and even source themes, do not involve research. Articles may have numerous footnotes and not be source studies. Studies with bibliographies may require no footnotes or even documentation in the text if they are simply uninterpreted reports of the findings. Page references are usually preferable, however. If your reader is familiar with a source, you may document some discussion of it without footnotes or page references. Miss Strauss is wise to supply them in her paper, which follows. A study like hers does not require compilation notes; in a study like Hart's they are indispensable.

Subjects for research may be found in many ways other than through the *Readers' Guide*. But when the subject is found in old sources, the investigator should do any research necessary to bring the study up to date to be sure that recent studies have not been published on the subject.

The papers which follow stress respectively the techniques of documentation, compilation, investigation, and quotation.

The Carson paper is a remarkably helpful model illustrating the devices for presenting a documented discussion. It is also styled to a widely accepted convention. The writer who follows it is likely to meet little disapproval of his work.

The Hart paper illustrates the extreme of a closely documented factual report. The short paragraphs indicate that this is report rather than discussion. The data are intricately organized, and the fluency of the sentence structure attests the assimilation of the detail to the author's purpose.

It would be hard to find a more beautiful illustration of the investigator's attitude than Topliff's paper. A sophomore in the School of Agriculture, preparing himself to enter the butter industry, Topliff in 1940 began the study with a natural bias against his competitor. But he weighed the facts with an open mind, and the result is a triumph of liberality over prejudice. His temperate statement of his competitor's case has been described by one reviewer as a "notable historical summary" of the controversy which has continued for sixty-four years.

Miss Strauss's paper, submitted for a course in literature, illustrates the difficult art of discriminate quotation. Here the commentary and the numerous quotations are woven in such a consistent line of development that the reader has no sense of digression or irrelevance.

Not every paper requires a table of contents. Miss Strauss's expert direction needs no additional guide. In the other three papers the tables are useful to the reader. Carson wished to bring out his analysis, and the outline is the appropriate form. Hart combines a chronological table with a geographical division suitable to his subject. Topliff felt that in his paper a list of the topics would be what the reader would want. In each case the author's objective results in a useful guide to the reading.

A

A MODEL FOR THE RESEARCH PAPER

The following paper, the work of a seventeen-year-old freshman, was written in 1943 and brought the history up to date at that time. The type and magnitude of the study make it a useful model in several important respects. The bibliography indicates reference to two books and thirteen periodicals. From these, twenty specific notes were used. The distribution of sources in the footnotes suggests independent organization on the part of the student writer. The exposition itself deserves praise for clarity in presenting its outline and for discrimination in introducing the sources into the text of the discussion. Note also the careful interpretation of the data. The paper has as its main content the information derived from reading. Note that it has taken three thousand words to correlate the data of twenty notes into a simple, straight-forward, unpadded report.

The table of contents is in outline form. It presents the divisions of the paper in logical series and is well proportioned to serve as a guide to the reading.

In its mechanics, this paper illustrates a widely accepted convention. An older, somewhat more formal style, illustrated by the Topliff paper (pages 96-109), is still preferred by many. The present trend, however, is toward simplification and economy. Some economies which are finding increasing acceptance are illustrated in the Gongwer paper (pages 43-50). The Carson paper represents the maximum economy generally favored for formal writing.

THE EFFECTIVENESS OF RADIO ADVERTISING

A Research Paper

by

John G. Carson

English 32—Division H
Miss Johnson
March 31, 1943
No. 15 (Outside)
Carson, John G.

Table of Contents

THE EFFECTIVENESS OF RADIO ADVERTISING

I. Early Radio Advertising

Although radio advertising is something which affects a great number of people in this country, very few of the general public know this form of advertising as anything but a disturber of nice quiet evenings at home. The general picture of the effectiveness of radio advertising may be arrived at by showing how this form of publicity developed, what it means to the advertiser in the form of expenditure, how the sponsor attempts to sell by radio, and finally how public reaction may be measured.

Advertising has done much toward improving radio, and this phase of improvement in broadcast quality must be taken into consideration before a discussion of the other effects of radio advertising is undertaken.

When radio was getting its start, all of the programs were sponsored by the station which broadcast them and their only purpose was to publicize the station. After several years of this sort of broadcasting, a different idea was evolved. Certain musical organizations decided to attempt a new venture by means of which classical music could be put on the air. The public was asked to send contributions to defray the costs of broadcast time and talent, but apparently the public was not interested at the time because all ventures of this nature, including one sponsored by a group of prominent bankers, failed.[1]

After the failure of the experiments at public sponsorship of radio programs, the radio stations opened their doors to advertisers who

---

[1] O. E. Dunlap, Jr., "Shall Advertising Be Given the Air?" Outlook, Vol. 141 (November 11, 1925), p. 387.

2

were willing to risk money on a new medium of publicity. The first commercially sponsored broadcast on a national network was aired on December 31, 1923, over the National Broadcasting Company under the sponsorship of the Victor Phonograph Company.[2] This program started a new form of advertising which has not yet reached its full development.

Early radio advertising consisted of merely announcing the name of the sponsor, but soon certain companies began to insert sales talks about their products into their programs and then public resentment started. One writer of 1924, expressing his opinion on the reaction of the public, said that the average person would turn the dial as soon as a direct advertisement started, but that in a short while there would be no escape because all stations would carry the same sort of thing.[3] This prediction almost came true, but a few companies refrained from selling their products over the air by direct advertising.

Early direct advertising by radio was resented by the radio industry itself as well as by the listening public. A report on the 1929 meeting of the National Association of Broadcasters states that this influential organization made a recommendation to the broadcasting industry that all commercial announcements be barred from programs after 6 P.M.[4] Although adoption of this reform probably would have increased the enjoyment of evening programs by tired working men,

---

[2] Irving Kolodin, "Propaganda on the Air," American Mercury, Vol. 35 (July, 1935), p. 298.

[3] J. C. Young, "How Will You Have Your Advertising?" Radio Broadcast, Vol. 6 (December, 1924), p. 246.

[4] Edgar H. Felix, "Regarding Direct Radio Advertising," Radio Broadcast, Vol. 15 (June, 1929), p. 73.

needless to say, it did not meet with the favor of advertisers who want to reach as large an audience as possible.

II. Costs of Radio Advertising

The great amounts of money spent on radio advertising by the sponsors of programs is an indication of the effect of radio commercials on the public. Companies have different ways of determining how their advertising is received by the listener, and these methods will be discussed in detail later, but the fact remains that sponsors do spend large sums of money on their programs; therefore one may conclude that they get some return on this expenditure or they would not stay in business. The two bills which the sponsor must pay are first, to the radio actors or other talent which he hires for the program; and second, to the radio station or network for the privilege of using broadcasting facilities.

The high salaries which radio stars receive are general knowledge and need not be dwelt on, but there is one rather unusual radio talent problem which is discussed in a book by two experts on radio broadcasting, Ivan E. Firth and Gladys S. Erskine. This problem is one that is brought about by the different time zones in this country. Since most radio programs are designed for a certain type of listener, a program aired over a national network might not reach the same type of listener in all parts of the country on account of the four-hour difference in time between New York and San Francisco. There are two ways to get the program to the listener at the right time, but neither is entirely satisfactory. The simplest and cheapest way is to have a recording of the program made and broadcast over stations in each time zone at the desired time. Many sponsors are adverse to

4

recorded programs, however; consequently they must rebroadcast the program in the different time zones by hiring local talent to perform. This is, of course, much more expensive than making a recording; therefore it is not a very common practice.[5]

After the sponsor of a commercial program has met the expense of hiring talent, he must pay for the broadcast time itself. When commercial broadcasting was getting its start, the radio stations did not charge terribly large amounts for the use of broadcasting facilities. In 1925 the highest rate for radio time was charged by station WEAF in New York which considered $500 an hour a reasonable rate.[6] Prices rose rapidly, however, and there was quite a change by 1932. In that year the rates charged by the Columbia Network for broadcast time were as high as $15,000 an hour for certain hours in the evening and somewhat less for daytime hours. A year of fifteen-minute programs broadcast six days a week cost the sponsor $27,000 a week.[7] This will give some idea of the great amount of money which the sponsors of daily "soap operas" spend for their advertising.

The great profits made by the radio networks in the early thirties show that advertisers certainly must have considered broadcasting an effective form of publicity. A reliable business magazine estimated that in 1930 one hundred millions of dollars were spent by advertisers for radio time alone and that fifty millions were spent for talent.

---

[5] Ivan E. Firth and Gladys S. Erskine, Gateway to Radio, pp. 183 f.

[6] Dunlap, p. 388.

[7] "Neither Sponsors nor Stations Heed Radio Listeners' Grumbling," Business Week, February 10, 1932, p. 19.

5

In the same article it was stated that the income of the National
Broadcasting Company was one-third higher in the first six months of
1931 than in the same period in 1930, and the income of the Columbia
Broadcasting System was up almost one-half.[8]   Gains like these in the
slim years of depression show us that radio was thriving.

Since radio advertising is the newest form of publicity, the other
advertising media, covered by the field of publishing, are of course
resentful of the amazing success which radio advertising has encoun-
tered.   This resentment has caused antagonism between published
and radio advertising which might almost be called a feud.   The
reason for this antagonism is apparent when one reads some figures in
Business Week.   In 1934 radio advertising did 35 per cent more business than in 1933 while magazine advertising did only 21 per cent more
and newspapers only 14 per cent more.[9]   Since a successful competitor
is resented in any field this same trait of human nature applies to
advertising.

The antagonism between publishers and radio has caused less
effective advertising, according to Mr. Firth and Miss Erskine.   They
claim that business could have much better advertising campaigns if
the different forms of advertising were in a cooperative mood, for an
agent could plan a much more coordinated campaign if this were the
case.   Cooperation among advertising media would therefore help to
improve business.[10]

---

[8] "Radio Advertising Headed for 150 Millions in 1931," Business
Week, August 12, 1931, p. 10.

[9] "Radio Against the Field," Business Week, January 12, 1935,
p. 12.

[10] Firth and Erskine, pp. 279 f.

6

One concern tried to ascertain the relative merits of broadcast and published advertising in 1935 by a telephone survey. According to the results of this survey, which was conducted to find out how many people actually could identify the sponsor of the program to which they were listening, the cost to the sponsor of the program was $16.22 for every thousand persons who were able to recognize the sponsor when questioned.

These results were welcome news to magazine publishers, for the cost of a one-page magazine advertisement has been estimated at between two and four dollars for every thousand readers. The radio advertisers have an answer for this, however, for they claim that every reader of the magazine does not read the advertisements.[11]

Since the surveys of this kind are not entirely accurate, one may not consider these figures as conclusive proof of the merits of either kind of publicity, but the results of the survey afford some basis for comparison.

III. Methods of Radio Advertising

The whole idea of advertising by radio is based on the same principle as the old-time medicine show, according to one radio authority. He compares the entertainment which is sent over the ether waves to the Indian, banjo player, and magician who made up the retinue of the patent medicine man. Continuing in the comparison, he says that the only purpose of the radio actor and musician is to put the people in a good humor so that the sponsor, who corresponds to the medicine man, will have a receptive audience when he

---

[11] "Press vs. Radio," Business Week, February 9, 1935, p. 10.

peddles his wares.[12]   Although this conception of radio seems a bit extreme at first glance, I believe that it is basically true, since all good advertising has to have something to attract the customers' attention.

There are several factors that influence the public's reception of radio advertising.   Perhaps the first factor is the nature of the product which the sponsor has to sell.   According to the two previously mentioned radio experts, Ivan E. Firth and Gladys S. Erskine, it has been found that articles connected with recreation are the easiest to sell by radio because the only possibility of building up ill-will in the minds of listeners is among non-users of the product whose business is no loss to the sponsor.

The unpleasant necessities of life such as tooth paste, corn plasters, and the like require more tactful advertising and are probably best sold by just using the publicity afforded by repetition of the trade name rather than by a detailed sales talk.[13]

The method of approach to the prospective buyer used in the commercial message is another factor that influences the listening public. The most common method in use today is the lowly "plug."   An article in a recent issue of Reader's Digest by one of the associate editors [14] of that magazine clearly summed up one of the most general attitudes toward the "plug" as taken in particular by an unusual organization which calls itself Plug Shrinkers.   The Plug Shrinkers feel that the American public is tired of hearing about all the aches

---

[12] J. T. Flynn, "Radio: Medicine Show," American Scholar, Vol. 7, No. 4 (October, 1938), pp. 433 f.

[13] Firth and Erskine, p. 28.

[14] Robert Littell, "Radio's Plug-Uglies," Reader's Digest, Vol. 41 (August, 1942), pp. 1-4.

8

and pains to which the human body is subject; consequently they decided to do something about radio advertising. In the article a great number of companies were criticized for poor taste in advertising and a few were praised for their high standards of commercials. Special reference was made to the very unpleasant ways in which certain concerns try to make their advertising timely by using the war as a selling point in their commercials. The enrollment blank of the organization, from which the following is taken, appears at the end of the article and shows very clearly the attitude of the Plug Shrinkers toward the commonest type of radio advertising:

> Dear Fellow Plug Shrinker: I am with you, heart, soul and offended ears. Enroll me as an Outraged Member.
>
> Please tell .... (give sponsor's or product's name) that his radio "commercials" are (check appropriate epithet) in bad taste ..... hokum ..... tiresome ..... repetitious ..... repulsive ..... long-winded ..... too intimate ..... too anatomical ..... silly ..... syrupy ..... poor sales policy .....
>
> I understand that this entitles me to enrollment as a Militant Member, in token whereof Plug Shrinkers will refrain from sending me one life-sized scientific drawing, reproduced in natural colors, of the contents of the Human Stomach after a hearty meal.
>
> Name ....
>
> Address ....
>
> City .... State ....

A report on the results of the Plug Shrinkers' campaign was given in a later issue of the Digest. In the first four weeks of the campaign 15,000 radio listeners sent in enrollment cards and many more followed. From the comments made in letters to Plug Shrinkers four lessons were found which might be useful to radio advertisers. The first lesson was not to use the war as a plug and the second was not to underestimate the intelligence of the American people. Another lesson for advertisers was that bad plugs drive customers away and the last lesson was that the length of plugs could be considerably cut down with no loss in effectiveness.[15] The large cross section of the American public which was represented among these letters clearly indicates to even the casual reader that these four lessons are not based on the opinions of a minority group; consequently the radio industry would be wise to heed the advice given by listeners.

An unusual type of radio advertising which bears mentioning is the "seal plan" of radio station WLW in Cincinnati, Ohio. This plan operates in a manner similar to the Good Housekeeping Seal of Approval system except that WLW does not test the products in a laboratory but uses the reactions of a small group of typical consumers as a basis for the guarantee. If this group of about a thousand housewives decides, after several months' trial of the product, that the sponsor advertises truthfully, then the sponsor may add to his commercial that "this product is approved by the WLW Consumer's Foundation."[16] The approval of a product by one group of housewives is a good selling point to all housewives; therefore one may conclude that the seal plan has potentialities for selling certain household goods.

------

[15] "Report on Plug Shrinkers," Reader's Digest, Vol. 41 (October, 1942), pp. 58-61.

[16] "WLW's Seal Plan," Business Week, November 15, 1941, p. 58.

10

IV. Results of Radio Advertising

There are different ways for determining how effective radio advertising is. Some of these are direct indications, and others are indirect methods which determine the size and character of the listening audience and draw conclusions as to the effectiveness of advertising from this information.

Probably the most important direct indicator of the effect of a program on the public is the fan mail received by the sponsor. The amount and kind of fan mail received by different companies varies tremendously of course; therefore it is impractical to include a lengthy discussion on fan mail. One or two examples of fan mail volume are sufficient to impress the importance of fan mail. As early as 1929 the Cities Service Company received five thousand letters a month and another concern had a mailing list of 150,000 made up of radio listeners who sent in fan mail.[17] Fan mail is also an aid to the sponsor in determining what the public likes and he may alter his program to suit public taste.

Listener surveys are an indirect way of finding how radio advertising affects the average American. Surveys of the effectiveness of radio are conducted by mail or telephone or by a special new device called the Audimeter. Since the first two types of survey are less accurate than the use of the Audimeter, I shall discuss the matter of surveys in terms of comparison with the Audimeter.

The development and operation of the Audimeter is described in a recent issue of Time magazine. This machine consists of a rotating

---

[17] Frank Presbrey, The History and Development of Advertising, p. 580.

11

drum with a stylus attachment that records every time that the radio is turned on or off or that the tuning dial is moved. The device was developed by the A. C. Nielsen Company of Chicago and the findings of the surveys made by the Audimeter are now used to make up the Nielsen Radio Index which is highly respected in the field of advertising. Since the Nielsen Company is in Chicago, the first tests of the Audimeter were made in the Middle West and the results were very interesting. It was found that the radios tested were played on an average of five and one-half hours a day and also that radios were used more in homes without telephones than in ones with phones. Another interesting fact that was discovered was that most of the radio audience turned off their radios after the star of a certain night program signed off, and consequently missed the last commercial.

This same article compares the effectiveness of the Audimeter surveys with the results of surveys conducted by Crossley and Hooper, the two most successful finders of fact about radio audiences. Since both Crossley and Hooper surveys are conducted by telephone, it is impossible for them to include the large rural radio audience which does not have telephones. The Audimeter does not have this drawback, however; therefore it can cover a truer cross section of the public. The only thing that the Audimeter cannot tell is whether the radio is being listened to or not.[18]

Another unusual indication of the scope of radio advertising has been found in an even more indirect way. At the time of the height of the popularity of Amos and Andy the telephone company reported a large drop in business during the fifteen minutes while this well-

[18] "Who Listens to What?" Time, Vol. 41 (January 4, 1943), p. 62.

12

known team was on the air.[19]   This fact shows very clearly, although
indirectly, what a tremendous number of potential buyers may be
reached by radio advertising.

In conclusion I quote a passage from Mr. Firth and Miss Erskine's
book which seems to sum up the existing need for more effective radio
advertising:

> Until the sponsors and all those responsible have a
> greater respect for the radio audience, which can only be
> achieved by that audience showing a greater respect for them-
> selves and for the programs brought into their homes, the
> full entertaining and cultural value of radio will not be
> obtained.[20]

---

[19] Firth and Erskine, p. 277.

[20] Ibid., p. 298.

13

Bibliography

Books

Firth, Ivan Eustace, and Erskine, Gladys Shaw. Gateway to Radio.
New York: The Macaulay Co., 1934.

Presbrey, Frank. The History and Development of Advertising.
Garden City, New York: Doubleday, Doran & Co., Inc., 1929.

Articles

Dunlap, O. E. Jr. "Shall Advertising Be Given the Air?" Outlook,
Vol. 141 (November 11, 1925), pp. 387-388.

Felix, Edgar H. "Regarding Direct Radio Advertising," Radio
Broadcast, Vol. 15 (June, 1929), p. 73.

Flynn, J. T. "Radio: Medicine Show," American Scholar, Vol. 7, No.
4 (October, 1938), pp. 430-437.

Kolodin, Irving. "Propaganda on the Air," American Mercury, Vol.
35 (July, 1935), pp. 293-300.

Littell, Robert. "Radio's Plug-Uglies," Reader's Digest, Vol. 41
(August, 1942), pp. 1-4.

"Neither Sponsors nor Stations Heed Radio Listeners' Grumbling,"
Business Week, February 10, 1932, pp. 18-19.

"Press vs. Radio," Business Week, February 9, 1935, p. 10.

"Radio Advertising Headed for 150 Millions in 1931," Business Week,
August 12, 1931, p. 10.

"Radio Against the Field," Business Week, January 12, 1935, p. 12.

"Report on Plug Shrinkers," Reader's Digest, Vol. 41 (October, 1942),
pp. 58-61.

"Who Listens to What?" Time, Vol. 41 (January 4, 1943), pp. 61-62.

"WLW's Seal Plan," Business Week, November 15, 1941, p. 58.

Young, J. C. "How Will You Have Your Advertising?" Radio Broadcast, Vol. 6 (December, 1924), pp. 244-250.

B

A CLOSELY DOCUMENTED
COMPILATION

As mentioned previously, the Carson paper requires three thousand words to correlate the data of twenty notes into a simple, straight-forward, unpadded report.

But it must not be supposed that the exposition invariably requires many words. The following paper is a noteworthy exception. Here the writer has used less than two thousand words to correlate more than fifty notes. There is little author comment, and most of the source reference is carried in the footnotes. The writer's task has been mainly one of organization and sentence structure, and the facts speak for themselves.

The Carson paper is the safer model as a general rule, but the following paper should also be examined carefully. Its purpose is to combine in one record every known detail of the story. The documentation is unusually close; Hart wished to be able to cite his authority and, if need be, return to the source in the event of any future question concerning the accuracy of the information.

Hart uses more than fifty notes in a report of less than two thousand words. Such intricate cross-reference could not have been managed without a good system of note taking. To reduce the space required for the footnotes, Hart has invented some economies of his own. Most of his short cuts, however, are to be found in agricultural publications. For his private purpose the reference is certainly clearer as it is.

Note Hart's principle of documentation: though the sources are described completely in the bibliography at the end, the sources cited on each page of the report are there also described in full. Thus the reader is spared troublesome cross-reference to other parts of the report. Hart also dispenses with the Latin abbreviations employed in other fields than agriculture.

Note the difference in the table of contents. Topliff considered an index to his topics most appropriate, whereas Carson preferred the outline. Hart combines a chronological table with a geographical division. In each case the writer's purpose is to furnish a useful guide to the reading.

The abbreviations used in describing documents in this paper are not those ordinarily found in print. The paper was prepared as a private record, and the abbreviations used were more intelligible to the writer for his own future reference. The important thing in all documentation is to suit the reader's needs. In this case, the writer himself was the reader.

The novice is advised to proceed cautiously in any experimentation with variants of form or economy in documentation. The convention must be appropriate to the purpose of the report. In general, the beginner writing his first paper is advised to follow the Carson report as his model.

THE SPREAD OF THE EUROPEAN CORN BORER
IN CANADA AND THE UNITED STATES

A Research Paper

by

John W. Hart

English 31—Division H
Miss Johnson
June 4, 1940
No. 8 (Outside)
Hart, John W.

Table of Contents

The Spread of the European Corn Borer
in Canada and the United States

CANADIAN INFESTATION

An exotic army could hardly have caused North America the expense which a foreign pest has effected. This pest is the European Corn Borer (Pyrausta nubilalis Hübn.). The entrance of the borer into this continent dates back to either 1909 or 1910. The insect is thought to have entered this country in shipments of broom corn from either Austria or Hungary. The larvae of the moths were hidden in corn imported by a broom factory at St. Thomas, Canada. Presence of the insect was discovered in 1920 at which time the insect was present in an area of 3,000 square miles.[1] This importation of the European Corn Borer occurred before the quarantine act of August 20, 1912.[2]

In 1920 in Essex and Kent counties, Canada, 127,000 acres of corn yielded over fifty bushels per acre.[3] Even in 1923 these counties showed a mere 3 per cent infestation;[1] but by 1926 the acreage in Kent and Essex had been reduced to 95,000 acres, and the yield had dropped to ten bushels per acre.[3] The average infestations per stalk were: in Essex, 83 per cent; in Kent, 78.7 per cent.[1]

After discovering the seriousness of the corn-borer problem, the Canadians started clean-up campaigns in Essex and Kent counties.

[1] J. J. Davis, L. Caesar, G. A. Ficht, S. R. Miles, "Report of European Corn Borer Symposium," p. 3.

[2] W. H. Larrimer, "America's Corn Crop and the Corn Borer," Scientific Monthly, Vol. 27, N '28, p. 424.

[3] T. U. H. Ellinger, "The Corn Borer Assassin of the Corn Field," Union Stock Yards Publication, pp. 3-4.

2

As a result of these efforts, the acreage and yield in these Canadian counties increased between 1927 and 1932.[1]

There was an infestation reported in 1920 in Welland County, Ontario, across the Niagara River from the New York infestation. Another area was reported along the shore of Lake Erie with the center at St. Thomas, Ontario. The second-mentioned infestation was reported to be larger than the Welland County infestation.[2]

At the close of 1924 there were 18,000 square miles of Canadian infested territory comprising the southern Ontario peninsula bordering Lake Erie. This area was practically continuous with the United States infestation.[3]

UNITED STATES INFESTATION

According to T. U. H. Ellinger in the publication The Corn Borer Assassin of the Corn Field, the first specimens of the borer were found in 1916, but they were not identified until the next year. D. J. Caffrey, an expert on the corn borer, in the Farmers' Bulletin 1046, also places the discovery in the year 1917. The insects probably entered the United States in much the same manner as they entered Canada. The shipments in which the larvae may have been hiding in hemp were imported from Europe by cordage factories. Between

---

[1] G. W. Collier, Lynn Robertson, "Adjusting Central Indiana Farming to Corn Borer Conditions," P. U. Ag. Ex. Stat. Bul. 389, Mar '34, p. 2.

[2] D. J. Caffrey, L. H. Worthley, "European Corn Borer; Its Present Status and Methods of Control," U.S.D.A. Far. Bul. 1548, O '27, p. 3.

[3] Caffrey, Worthley, "A Progress Report on the Investigations of the European Corn Borer," U.S.D.A. Bul. 1476, F '27, p. 13.

3

the years of 1909 and 1914, 12,000 tons of broom corn were imported into this country.[1] It is thought that the borers entered either Evert, Massachusetts, or Amsterdam, New York.[2]

The first infestation in the United States in all probability did not come to us from Canada. The method of infestation is not definitely known.

When it was first discovered, the corn borer was occupying thirty-four townships in Massachusetts, an area of 320 square miles, all of which was west, north, and northeast of Boston.[3] Stewart C. Vinal of Massachusetts discovered the corn borer's presence and started to study the insect. The borer caused extensive damage in the sweet corn in the area of its discovery.[4]

From the state of introduction, the insect soon spread to New York. The pest was discovered in eastern New York, January 1919, by F. V. Osterhoudt in his garden. Scouts showed that there was a widespread infestation in the regions surrounding Schenectady and portions of the Mohawk and Hudson River valleys.[5] At the reporting of the infestation there was an area of 400 square miles infested in New York.[3]

---

[1] D. J. Caffrey, L. H. Worthley, "A Progress Report on the Investigations of the European Corn Borer," U.S.D.A. Bul. 1476, F '27, p. 13.

[2] Caffrey, Worthley, "European Corn Borer; Its Present Status and Methods of Control," U.S.D.A. Far. Bul. 1548, O '27, p. 4.

[3] Caffrey, "The European Corn Borer," U.S.D.A. Far. Bul. 1046, Ap '19, pp. 4-5.

[4] W. H. Larrimer, "America's Corn Crop and the Corn Borer," Scientific Monthly, Vol. 27, N '28, p. 424.

[5] Same as 1, p. 11.

4

The first survey of any consequence was confined to Erie County and to Hanover town, Chautauqua County.[1] In 25 square miles (700 acres of corn) the average infestation was 21 per cent.[2]

In 1921 there were 5,550 plants examined; 30.8 per cent were infested. The average number of larvae was two and one-tenth per plant.[2] Twice as many plants were examined in 1922; the percentage decreased from 30.8 to 18, the number of larvae per 100 plants dropping from sixty-five to thirty-three.[3]

In 1923 in New York the percentage of stalk infestation decreased from 18 to 15. This was an average of thirty fields. The number of larvae per plant dropped from thirty-three in 1921 to nineteen in 1923.[3] By 1924, in spite of this decrease in population, 2,882 square miles were infested in New York.[4]

In the years of 1924, 1925, and 1926 the number of larvae increased from 68 to 242 larvae per 100 plants; but since 1927 the population has dropped to 197 per 100 plants.[5]

Such a pest as the European Corn Borer could hardly be satisfied merely with the devastation of the Canadian corn crop. The pest moved from Canada into the rich fields of American corn where it threatened to cut the life line of the mid-western farmers if it remained unchecked. The entrance was probably by flight.

---

[1] H. N. Bartley, L. B. Scott, "Preliminary Report upon the Infestation and General Status of the European Corn Borer in Western New York," U.S.D.A. Cir. N.S. 197, D '31, p. 1.

[2] Same as 1, p. 6.

[3] Same as 1, p. 7.

[4] D. J. Caffrey, L. H. Worthley, "A Progress Report on the Investigations of the European Corn Borer," U.S.D.A. Bul. 1476, F '27, p. 11.

[5] Same as 1, pp. 7-9.

5

The infested area known as the Erie Section embraces land in Ohio, Michigan, Pennsylvania, and New York. During the summer of 1921, the insect was found in an island in Lake Erie seven miles from Ohio.[1] The island is Middle Bass Island.[2] By 1924 the insect was established in most of the American territory along Lake Erie.[3]

In 1922 there was a sparse but extensive infestation of the corn borer reported throughout a narrow strip of territory comprising most of the townships bordering Lake Erie in the states of Michigan, Ohio, Pennsylvania, and New York.[2] In 1922 the borer occupied 7,896 square miles in the United States. This was all in three sections:[4]

1. Massachusetts and Connecticut infestation
2. New York area
3. American side of Lake Erie

By 1924 the area of infestation:[1]

1. 4,812 square miles in Western New York
2. 6,591 square miles in Northern Ohio
3. 1,999 square miles in Northwestern Pennsylvania
4. 2,828 square miles in Southeastern Michigan

16,230 square miles in Lake Erie Section

The first state infested with the corn borer was Massachusetts where the pest came in 1916.[5]

-----

[1] D. J. Caffrey, L. H. Worthley, "A Progress Report on the Investigations of the European Corn Borer," U.S.D.A. Bul. 1476, F '27, p. 11-12.

[2] Caffrey, Worthley, "European Corn Borer; Its Present Status and Methods of Control," U.S.D.A. Far. Bul. 1548, O '27, p. 2.

[3] Same as 1, p. 12.

[4] Caffrey, Worthley, "The European Corn Borer and Its Control," U.S.D.A. Far. Bul. 1294, '22, p. 2.

[5] T. U. H. Ellinger, "The Corn Borer Assassin of the Corn Field," Union Stock Yards Publication, p. 14.

6

In 1919 the European Corn Borer entered the states of New York and Pennsylvania.[1]   The New York infestation was discovered on the farm of Alfred Morrison in Erie County, New York.[2]   In Erie County, Pennsylvania, the pest occupied 32 square miles in 1919.[3]

The corn borer entered New Hampshire, Maine, and Rhode Island in either 1920 or 1921.[1]   There was no increase in the spread of the insect in Pennsylvania in the year of 1921.[3]

Ohio and Michigan were victimized by the European scourge in 1921 for the first time.[1]   While these two states were being introduced to the European Corn Borer, Erie County in Pennsylvania was subjected to an increase from 32 square miles to 302 square miles of corn-borer infested territory.[3]

There was little new territory touched in 1922, but the borer made great gains in the state of Pennsylvania where the amount of infested territory was more than doubled.   The infestation was reported to cover 613 square miles of the state.   All of this extended over Erie and Crawford counties.[3]

According to J. J. Davis, by 1923 two more states were added to the list of areas in which the corn borer was working; these states were Vermont and Connecticut.[1]   Caffrey and Worthley had previously reported Connecticut as infested in 1922.

The European pest made little progress in Pennsylvania in the year of 1923.   In occupying 653 square miles the borer gained only

---

[1] J. J. Davis, "The European Corn Borer: Past, Present, and Future," J. Econ. Entom., Vol. 28, No. 2, Ap '35, p. 324.

[2] D. J. Caffrey, L. H. Worthley, "A Progress Report on the Investigations of the European Corn Borer," U.S.D.A. Bul. 1476, F '27, p. 11.

[3] T. L. Guyton, P. G. Brown, "European Corn Borer in Pennsylvania," Pa. Dept. of Agri. Bul., Vol. 11, No. 15, D '28, p. 4.

7

40 square miles over the 1922 infestation.[1]

In 1924 or 1925 the European Corn Borer did not enter any state previously uninfested. In 1924 the Pennsylvania infestation increased from 653 square miles to 1,999 square miles. Two new counties, never before touched, were infested in 1924; they were Mercier and Warren. The spread in the year following 1924 was very great; ten new counties were infested in Pennsylvania alone.[1]

The year of 1926 was a red letter one for the European scourge. New Jersey, West Virginia, and Indiana were all infested.[2] The first Indiana infestation included six northeastern counties: Stuben, De Kalb, Allen, Lagrange, Noble, and Whitley.[3] The spread was great, and it covered thirty-nine townships in Indiana by the end of 1926.[4] The borer was discovered in Illinois in December, 1926.[5] The specimen found in Illinois was found in Yellow Head Township, Kankakee County. At the close of 1926 there were two large areas of occupation in the United States. These occupied 93,000 square miles.[6]

———

[1] T. L. Guyton, P. G. Brown, "European Corn Borer in Pennsylvania," Pa. Dept. of Agri. Bul., Vol. 11, No. 15, D '28, p. 4.

[2] J. J. Davis, "The European Corn Borer: Past, Present, and Future," J. Econ. Entom., Vol. 28, No. 2, Ap '35, p. 324.

[3] G. A. Ficht, "The European Corn Borer in Indiana," P. U. Ag. Ex. Stat. Bul. 406, Jan '36, p. 3.

[4] H. J. Reed, "European Corn Borer Menaces Indiana's Most Important Crop," P. U. Ag. Ex. Stat. Cir. 178, Jan '31, p. 3.

[5] A. G. Ruggles, A. C. Arny, "European Corn Borer," Minn. U. Ag. Ext. Spec. Bul. 116, O '27, p. 2.

[6] D. J. Caffrey, L. H. Worthley, "European Corn Borer: Its Present Status and Methods of Control," U.S.D.A. Far. Bul. 1548, O '27, p. 2.

8

In the year 1926 the borers doubled in number in New York, and in Ohio, Michigan, and Pennsylvania the numbers increased by five times.[1]

Between 1925 and 1929 the corn borer gained a good foothold in Pennsylvania. At the close of 1929 the insect occupied forty-nine counties in the state. This was a very impressive growth.[2]

Kentucky was the only state in which a new infestation was reported in 1930.[3] In Indiana 303 townships were reported infested by 1930, whereas only thirty-nine were occupied in 1926.[4]

Two more states were added to the list of victims of the European Corn Borer in 1931. These states were Virginia and Wisconsin.[3]

In 1932, as in 1930, only one state reported first infestation; this state was Maryland.[3] The seriousness of the corn-borer problem to the American farmer becomes evident when one considers the fact that 140,000 square miles of good farm land were occupied by the corn borer in 1932.[5]

The last state reporting a new infestation (until 1935) was Delaware. This state reported the pest present in 1934. At the close

---

[1] T. U. H. Ellinger, "The Corn Borer Assassin of the Corn Field," Union Stock Yards Publication, p. 16.

[2] H. E. Hodgkiss, "The European Corn Borer," Pa. State College Ag. Ex. Stat. Cir. 128, Au '29, p. 3.

[3] J. J. Davis, "The European Corn Borer: Past, Present, and Future," J. Econ. Entom., Vol. 28, No. 2, Ap '35, p. 324.

[4] H. J. Reed, "European Corn Borer Menaces Indiana's Most Important Crop," P. U. Ag. Ex. Stat. Cir. 178, Jan '31, p. 3.

[5] G. W. Collier, Lynn Robertson, "Adjusting Central Indiana Farming to Corn Borer Conditions," P. U. Ag. Ex. Stat. Bul. 389, Mar '34, p. 3.

9

of 1934 surveys showed that the borer was making great progress; the area of American land occupied by this European pest was 246,721 square miles.[1]

The spread of the corn borer in Indiana has been very rapid. Since its entrance into this state in 1926, the corn borer has spread over a great portion of the state. In 1935 the pest was present in more than one-half of the counties of the state.[2]

The spread of the European Corn Borer has been rapid since it entered the United States in 1916. This menace to our corn crop has not been allowed to spread freely, but nevertheless, the pest now occupies a great portion of our very good corn land. The borer will probably continue to spread in the future, but control measures tend to lessen the severity of the attacks.

---

[1] J. J. Davis, "The European Corn Borer: Past, Present, and Future," J. Econ. Entom., Vol. 28, No. 2, Ap '35, p. 324.

[2] G. A. Ficht, "The European Corn Borer in Indiana," P. U. Ag. Ex. Stat. Bul. 406, Jan '36, p. 3.

10

Bibliography

Bartley, H. N., and L. B. Scott. "Preliminary Report upon the Infestation and General Status of the European Corn Borer in Western New York." U.S.D.A. Cir. N.S. 197, D '31.

Caffrey, D. J. "The European Corn Borer." U.S.D.A. Far. Bul. 1046, Ap '19.

Caffrey, D. J., and L. H. Worthley. "The European Corn Borer and Its Control." U.S.D.A. Far. Bul. 1294, '22.

"European Corn Borer: Its Present Status and Methods of Control." U.S.D.A. Far. Bul. 1548, O '27.

"A Progress Report on the Investigations of the European Corn Borer." U.S.D.A. Bul. 1476, F '27.

Collier, G. W., and Lynn Robertson. "Adjusting Central Indiana Farming to Corn Borer Conditions." P. U. Ag. Ex. Stat. Bul. 389, Mar '34.

Davis, J. J. "The European Corn Borer: Past, Present, and Future." J. Econ. Entom., Vol. 28, No. 2, Ap '35.

Davis, J. J., and L. Caesar, G. A. Ficht, and S. R. Miles. "Report of European Corn Borer Symposium." Purdue Agricultural Conference, 1931. (Private Copy.)

Ellinger, T. U. H. "The Corn Borer Assassin of the Corn Field." Union Stock Yards Publication, [ca. 1927].

Ficht, G. A. "The European Corn Borer in Indiana." P. U. Ag. Ex. Stat. Bul. 406, Jan '36.

Guyton, T. L., and P. G. Brown. "European Corn Borer in Pennsylvania." Pa. Dept. of Agri. Bul., Vol. 11, No. 15, D '28.

Hodgkiss, H. E. "The European Corn Borer." Pa. State College Ag. Ex. Stat. Cir. 128, Au '29.

Larrimer, W. H. "America's Corn Crop and the Corn Borer." Scientific Monthly, Vol. 27, N '28, pp. 424-33.

Reed, H. J. "European Corn Borer Menaces Indiana's Most Important Crop." P. U. Ag. Ex. Stat. Cir. 178, Jan '31.

Ruggles, A. G. and A. C. Arny. "European Corn Borer." Minn. U. Ag. Ext. Spec. Bul. 116, O '27.

C

AN INVESTIGATION OF A CONTROVERSIAL SUBJECT

The author of the following paper was a sophomore in the School of Agriculture, preparing himself to enter the butter industry. He entered upon the study of the oleo problem with the natural bias of a competitor. But he also entered with an investigator's mind, determined to suspend judgment until the facts were known.

In that same year, 1940, this paper was included in a manual [1] copyrighted in mimeographed form. Thus it found its way to the Library of Congress. Nine years later, in the spring of 1949, a letter came from Washington requesting a copy of the pamphlet containing this student's report. Thus the student's work found its place in the nation's oleomargarine research.

An anonymous reviewer recommends this paper "as a notable historical summary of the oleo problem that culminated in congressional action in 1950, when repeal of the oleo tax climaxed a 64-year controversy on this vital subject."

The documentation is left as it was in 1940. The abbreviation *op. cit.* (*opere citato* is Latin for "in the work mentioned") means that the work has been mentioned in a previous footnote. *Op. cit.* is less in use now than formerly but is still widely favored, particularly in publication.

---

[1] Ellen Johnson, "The Research Paper," Mimeographed pamphlet privately copyrighted, 1940.

OLEOMARGARINE: FALSE COMPETITION AND
ITS RESULTS

A Research Paper

by

Marion C. Topliff

English 31-Division H
Miss Johnson
April 22, 1940
No. 8 (Outside)
Topliff, Marion C.

Table of Contents

Oleomargarine: False Competition and Its Results

"Oleomargarine manufacturers always look under the bed before retiring, lest a representative of the dairy industry be lurking there for no good purpose." [1] This statement indicates the high distrust that oleomargarine manufacturers have for the butter makers and their associates. They rightfully hold the butter trade in this distrust, for ever since oleomargarine was discovered in the nineteenth century, the dairy industry has been their closest and most active rival. If it had not been for the fact that oleomargarine competes with other products, especially butter, its invention would be more generally emphasized as one of the great scientific contributions to human welfare.[2] As it is, the oleomargarine trade has always been under a great number of stresses and strains as a result of competition, unfair and otherwise, and for a while did well to hold its own in the business world. The butter industry is the main source of this competition. The false and unfair competition against oleomargarine for which the dairy industry is responsible takes several forms. Some forms are hidden; some are plainly evident. Several of these forms will be described and their effects and results in the industry noted.

Although the butter and the oleomargarine industries do produce similar products, use similar equipment, use farm products as raw materials, and put their products through about the same amount of processing, the one has always been considered agricultural and the

---

[1] "Oleomargarine Faces New Attack," Business Week, No. 446 (March 19, 1938), p. 31.

[2] J. S. Abbott, Oleomargarine, Its Purity, Wholesomeness and Economic Importance (Washington: Institute of Margarin Manufacturers, 1922), p. 15.

2

other as industrial.[3] This belief has been built up falsely by oleomargarine competitors from the time oleomargarine was discovered but
is now, perhaps, beginning to subside a little. The realization that
oleomargarine, as well as butter, is also a farm product has been aided
by the legislation enacted concerning it and also by the continuous
fight between the two industries. Laws have been enacted in some
states requiring that the ingredients used in the finished product be
printed on the carton. Of course this legislation was designed originally to hinder rather than help the oleomargarine manufacturers as
well as to show the purity of the product. It has, however, aided
oleomargarine to some extent in that it makes the fact that oleomargarine comes as a product of the farm easier for the consumer to see
by putting the facts constantly before his eyes. In spite of the fact
that this supposed difference between the two industries has served
as one of the bases on which restraint of competition between the two
products has been maintained,[4] according to the Scientific American,
"Oleomargarine is as much a farm product as beef or butter, and is
as wholesome as either." [5]

Another point of similarity between oleomargarine and butter
which is sometimes stated as a difference is in their nutritive qualities.
Oleomargarine, when colored, has the appearance of butter, but, until
within the last few years, the dairy interests were justified in their claim

[3] William Richard Pabst, Butter and Oleomargarine (New York:
Columbia University Press, 1937), p. 28.

[4] Ibid., p. 28.

[5] Margarine Laws of Oregon and Washington Repealed by a
Referendum Vote of the People, November 4, 1924 (Washington: Institute of Margarine Manufacturers, 1925), p. 12.

3

that oleomargarine lacked some of the nutritive qualities of butter. Until recently one nutritional handicap of oleomargarine was that it lacked vitamin A, the vitamin which is contained in animal fats such as butter. Some manufacturers have overcome this deficiency by the addition, during the manufacturing process, of a product rich in vitamin A. Vitamin D is also contained in this preparation.[6] As a result oleomargarine need no longer lag behind butter in the vitamin nutrition it contains. Consequently, this point of nutritional deficiency as compared with butter is false and should no longer be used as an argument against oleomargarine.

The fact that oleomargarine manufacturers have not always been wholly successful in making their product resemble butter has no doubt in part been due to adverse legislation.[7] This is an unfortunate circumstance. As times become harder, people buy more oleo in relation to butter because it sells for about half the price of butter.[8] Now one way to make up a vitamin deficiency is to increase the consumption of the appropriate foodstuffs, such as milk, butter, eggs, meat, and vegetables, but this would add a considerable sum to the budget of a working class family of four or five people. On the other hand, recent research has made possible the addition of vitamins to foodstuffs, thereby making it possible to give the consumer an

---

[6] "Accepted Brands of Oleomargarine," Hygeia, Vol. XVII, No. 4 (April, 1939), p. 353.

[7] Carl L. Alsberg and Alonzo E. Taylor, The Fats and Oils: A General View (Stanford University, California: Stanford University Press, 1928), p. 76.

[8] R. L. Buell, "Death by Tariff," Fortune, Vol. XVIII, No. 2 (August, 1938), p. 34.

4

optimum intake at very low cost. Margarine is already treated in this manner.[9] Margarine so treated therefore serves as a valuable source of vitamins for the classes who cannot afford the more expensive products. The fact that oleomargarine thus serves a good purpose is, consequently, a reason for arguments against unfavorable legislation. The truth is that the manufacturers should be encouraged to make their product resemble butter more closely and thus increase the attractiveness of this valuable low-cost food. Legislation, therefore, hinders the development of an important product in that difficulty is experienced in making oleomargarine resemble butter in taste, color, and spreading qualities.[10]

The question of legislation logically brings up government regulation. No other industries except those making alcoholic liquors and narcotic drugs have been so "bound about with laws and regulations, licenses and taxes." [11] That the margarine industry has managed to survive at all in the years it has been harried by the government points to the inherent vitality of the business and the natural demand for its product.[12] Of course there is no argument against the fact that a nation has a right to protect its own industries by levying taxes upon the products of the competitive industries of foreign countries or by the outright prohibition of those products. No one, on the other hand, has "ever advocated the policy of prohibiting the sale of

[9] Dr. Emil Collett, "Vitaminising Foodstuffs," Food Manufacture, Vol. XV, No. 1 (January 5, 1940), p. 21.

[10] Alsberg and Taylor, op. cit., p. 76.

[11] "Oleomargarine Faces New Attack," op. cit., p. 26.

[12] Ibid., p. 31.

5

any useful and necessary consumable commodity to protect another commodity produced" in the same nation.[13]   This is exactly what has been done, nevertheless, in the attempts to prevent the sales of oleomargarine and further those of butter.   But first, how did all this legislation come about?   What started it in the first place?

In the last half of the nineteenth century chemical inventiveness began to outdistance business ethics, and by 1880 many newly developed substitutes for butter were used for adulteration and sold as the genuine article.   Not only butter but also products such as milk, cheese, flour, tea, coffee, honey, and olive oil were also adulterated. The adulteration of dairy products became exceedingly subtle.   Butter and cheese were filled with lard and water; oleo was sold as butter. Dairy farmers in New York, encouraged by public sentiment against the adulteration of products and also by early legislation against fraud, won support against the introduction of oleomargarine, a product easily substituted for butter.   Consequently legislation against oleomargarine became commonly accepted as a necessary part of the legislation against fraud.[14]   The dairy interests easily laid the blame for many of the farmer's troubles to the fraudulent sale of oleomargarine and its use in the adulteration of butter.   The depression of the late Seventies and the early Eighties had tempted the farmer to point to the new product as the cause of the trouble.[15]   Naturally, the adulteration and fraud connected with other products was just as

[13] Abbott, op. cit., p. 15.

[14] Pabst, op. cit., p. 29.

[15] Ibid., p. 30.

6

important, though the dairy industry took advantage of this one particular point.

In 1886 Congress imposed the first taxes and licenses on oleomargarine for its manufacture and sale.[16] This caused great readjustment in the industry. Concentration came as a result of the manufacturers' tax and "paved the way, eventually, for a great but gradual improvement in the welfare of the industry."[17] It is interesting to note that this legislation, designed partly to favor the dairy industry, had the effect of weeding out the smaller oleomargarine firms[18] and of establishing the industry on a more solid foundation; furthermore, research chemists were hired by the larger firms.[19] Yet, whatever incidental good may have come of it all, the fact remains that no butter manufacturer has to have a federal license to make butter, but the oleomargarine manufacturer pays a six hundred dollar fee per year, and the wholesalers and retailers of the product pay taxes and license fees far out of proportion to the value of the product. The main purpose of this legislation is to guard against fraud, but this aim could have been accomplished more effectively and honestly in a pure food and drug law. This legislation has come to be regarded chiefly as a means of protecting the dairy farmer against internal competitors.[20]

An example of recent government action against oleomargarine is the complaint of the Federal Trade Commission to the John F. Jelke

[16] Buell, op. cit., p. 34.

[17] Pabst, op. cit., p. 34.

[18] Ibid., p. 32.

[19] Ibid., p. 34.

[20] Buell, op. cit., p. 34.

7

Company, margarine manufacturers, instructing them to refrain from using the words "churn, churned, churnery" as applied to their product.[21] The Jelke people refused because the margarine manufacturing equipment is listed by its makers and purchased by its users as churns.[22] Most probably the dairy interests were behind these complaints. The oleomargarine makers are again the victims of a government-backed check on competition, and false at that, for margarine manufacturing equipment is rightfully named a "churn" in view of the fact that each type of margarine made in the United States is made by churning fats and oils in ripened milk or cream.[23] Therefore, what is more fitting than to use the terms connected with churning in the sale of their product? The dairy industry does. The oleomargarine makers should not be unfairly discriminated against.

In addition to the national government regulations the state governments have also imposed strict regulations on the oleomargarine industry. Continuous efforts have been made to legislate oleomargarine out of existence by laws designed to make the industry unprofitable. These laws never specifically prohibit the manufacture and sale of the product; they would probably be unconstitutional if they did so. Instead, the legislative strategy has been to enact a law taxing margarine or taxing retail dealers so much to sell margarine that they cannot afford to sell it. For example, in Montana a law was passed in 1927 imposing on retailers a tax of three hundred dollars per year

[21] "Oleomargarine Faces New Attack," op. cit., p. 26.

[22] Ibid., p. 31.

[23] J. S. Abbott, The Food Value of Margarin or Oleomargarine (Washington: Institute of Margarin Manufacturers, 1921), p. 6.

8

to sell the product.   That stopped its retail sales in Montana.[24]

This type of state tariff, that is, taxes and license fees, is raising interstate hostility.   Cottonseed oil is the chief ingredient of margarine as made by most companies other than meat packers.   A goodwill tour of Wisconsin businessmen, intended to further the use of the state's dairy products in the South, was abandoned because of the hostility of the southern natives.   The thirteen cotton-growing states then sent their own delegates to Wisconsin to notify the administration that "unless the bars were lowered to oleomargarine, they would produce a few tariffs of their own against butter" and other Wisconsin products.[25]   This brings out the obvious interstate hostility that has arisen between the dairy and oleomargarine industries.

This hostility is further shown in the case of the attempt made on April 15, 1938, to strike out the provision which had been in the appropriation bill since 1931 requiring that none of the funds of the Veterans' Administration be used for purchasing oleomargarine for anything but cooking use.   The strength of the dairy industry is indicated by the fact that the attempt was defeated and the provision remained in the bill.   However, in connection with the debate on the bill Senator "Cotton Ed" Smith said, "Have we come to the point where we are applying a high protective tariff between industries within our country?"   Senator Connally remarked, "I thought the war between the states was over in 1865."   Senator Bankhead contributed to the argument by saying, "The people of Wisconsin ought to be satisfied to

---

[24] J. S. Abbott, False Advertising (Washington: Institute of Margarine Manufacturers, 1928), p. 21.

[25] "Oleomargarine Faces New Attack," op. cit., p. 32.

9

sell their great appealing commodity upon its merits in the free market of the country, without coming to Congress and asking for a congressional condemnation of one of the competitors which they must meet in the free market of the country." [26] This last statement, directed at Wisconsin which is essentially a dairying state, indicates the obvious lengths to which the dairy faction will go to prevent the sale of oleomargarine.

The fact was stated at the beginning of this paper that the members of the oleomargarine industry were justified in their distrust of the butter and dairy industry. This view is supported by the citations of unfair means and false points of competition backed by the butter manufacturers. From all this one might expect as a natural consequence that the oleomargarine industry, under the pressure of these stresses and strains created by the initiative of the dairy industry, would gradually decrease in the volume of its business and eventually almost cease to exist. This is not the actual case. According to The Book of the Dairy, published in 1896, "Good margarine is quite capable of entering into successful competition with poor kinds of butter, but not with first-class butter, so that there can be no talk of a serious blow being dealt to the butter trade or to dairying through its use." [27] Recent actions of the dairy trade against margarine do not seem to agree with this. If they do agree, why should the dairy industry fight the margarine trade so energetically? In 1928, according to the Stanford University food research institute, butter has some competition

---

[26] Buell, op. cit., p. 34.

[27] W. Fleischmann, The Book of the Dairy, trans. C. M. Aikman and R. Patrick Wright (London: Blackie & Son, Ltd., [1896]), p. 322.

10

from margarine, "but unless existing conditions and legislation change greatly it is not likely soon to become much more severe." [28] Notice that legislation, implied to be restrictive in form, was a point in this quotation. Even against protectionist methods, oleomargarine consumption increased from 265,000,000 pounds to 390,000,000 pounds between 1934 and 1936. The proportion of oleomargarine to creamery butter went up from fifteen to twenty-four per cent.[29]

The cause of oleomargarine is justified but is not secure. The facts indicate that the butter industry has long fought the oleomargarine industry with its utmost strength, using both fair means and unfair tactics to prevent the spread of the popularity and the sales of oleomargarine. In spite of this, the margarine industry has constantly improved its product and is steadily increasing its sales. The natural demand for the product is evidently stronger than the preventive forcefulness of the dairy industry.

[28] Alsberg and Taylor, op. cit., p. 55.

[29] Buell, op. cit., p. 34.

Bibliography

Abbott, J. S. False Advertising. Washington: Institute of Margarine
Manufacturers, 1928.

———. The Food Value of Margarin or Oleomargarine. Washington: Institute of Margarin Manufacturers, 1921.

———. Oleomargarine, Its Purity, Wholesomeness and Economic
Importance. Washington: Institute of Margarin Manufacturers,
1922.

"Accepted Brands of Oleomargarine." Hygeia, Vol. XVII, No. 4
(April, 1939), pp. 353-354.

Alsberg, Carl L., and Alonzo E. Taylor. The Fats and Oils: A General
View. ("Fats and Oils Studies," No. 1, Food Research Institute,
Stanford University, California.) Stanford University Press, 1928.

Buell, R. L. "Death by Tariff; The Dairy Industry Raises Its Defenses." Fortune, Vol. XVIII, No. 2 (August, 1938), pp. 33-34.

Collett, Dr. Emil. "Vitaminising Foodstuffs." Food Manufacture.
Vol. XV, No. 1 (January 5, 1940), pp. 19-21.

Fleischmann, W. The Book of the Dairy. Trans. C. M. Aikman and
R. Patrick Wright. London: Blackie & Son, Ltd., [1896].

Margarine Laws of Oregon and Washington Repealed by a Referendum Vote of the People, November 4, 1924. Washington: Institute of Margarine Manufacturers, 1925.

"Oleomargarine Faces New Attack." Business Week. No. 446
(March 19, 1938), pp. 26 and 31-32.

Pabst, William Richard. Butter and Oleomargarine. New York:
Columbia University Press, 1937.

12

Supplementary Bibliography

Abbott, J. S. The Composition and Food Value of Margarine. Washington: Institute of Margarine Manufacturers, 1927.

Clayton, William. Margarine. New York: Longmans, Green & Co., 1920.

"Kraft in Oleo Fight." Business Week. No. 426 (October 30, 1937), p. 52.

"Kraft's Oleo Move; Food Company Sees Margarine as Natural Addition to Line." Business Week. No. 428 (November 13, 1937), pp. 43-44.

"Margarine Spoilage." Food Industries, Vol. II, No. 4 (April, 1939), pp. 238-239.

Opinions of Educators and Statesmen on Margarine and Margarine Legislation. Washington: Institute of Margarine Manufacturers, 1925.

Richardson, William D. The Economics of Vitamines. Washington: Institute of Margarine Manufacturers, 1927.

————. The Vitamine Doctrine and the Oleomargarine Industry. Washington: Institute of Margarin Manufacturers, 1921.

————. Vitamines Up to Date. Washington: Institute of Margarine Manufacturers, 1924.

"Vitaminizing of Margarine." American Journal of Public Health. Vol. XXVII, No. 12 (December, 1937), p. 1226.

D

A CRITICAL DISCUSSION

In the reading of books, questions arise that cannot be answered by arguing back and forth from the opponents' memories of past reading. Impressions are biased, or there would be no difference of opinion. The thing to do is to open the book and listen to what the author is actually saying on the subject.

This is one type of paper in which copious quotation is a merit. Only by throwing into relief the passages bearing upon the point can the question be settled. Miss Strauss has handled the problem with interest and clarity.

One must use discretion in presenting quotation from material protected by copyright. Generally, a few lines may be used freely—with full acknowledgment, of course; but before any extended quotation is circulated, it is advisable to ask permission of the copyright owner. Often permission is freely granted, but sometimes a fee is required. (Even a short poem, for example, may require a royalty for its general circulation.) As to the quotations in the following paper, Maugham's publishers have granted permission for their inclusion in this text.

The important thing in citing quotation is that it be *discriminate*. As a general rule, this means that little direct quotation is used. One quotes because the point is particularly well expressed or because one wishes to present the statement exactly as it appears in the source. In the following paper, that meant copious quotation. This paper is a distinct exception to the rule.

PHILIP'S SELF- TORTURE

by

Nancy Strauss

In Maugham's <u>Of Human Bondage</u> the question of Philip's self-torture or masochism is an interesting problem to consider. Philip's self-torture begins early in the book when he is still a young boy and continues until he is a mature man.

Although it may seem like a minor incident, Philip's relationship with his school friend Rose illustrates an early example of his tendencies. At first their friendship progresses well. Later, however, "He watched jealously Rose's companionship with others; and though he knew it was unreasonable could not help sometimes saying bitter things to him.... Not seldom Philip, knowing all the time how stupid he was, would force a quarrel, and they would not speak to one another for a couple of days." [1]

In spite of the fact that Philip would invariably apologize, it was an unnecessary test of their friendship. This was the first in a long line of Philip's tendencies toward self-torture. Later when their friendship seemed to be over, it was again Philip who provided the final blow. When Rose tried to "effect a reconciliation," Philip replied with "You bore me." [2]

Again "He did not know why he had answered in that fashion.

---

[1] Modern Library edition, p. 86. [The quotations in this paper are presented, by permission, from: **Of Human Bondage** by W. Somerset Maugham. Copyright 1915, 1936 by Doubleday & Co., Inc. —Editor.]

[2] P. 90.

2

He would have given anything to be friends with Rose. He hated to
have quarreled with him, and now that he saw he had given him
pain he was sorry. But at the moment he had not been master of
himself. It seemed that some devil had seized him, forcing him to
say bitter things against his will, even though at the time he wanted
to shake hands with Rose and meet him more than half-way. The
desire to wound had been too strong for him. He had wanted to
revenge himself for the pain and the humiliation he had endured.
It was pride: it was folly too, for he knew that Rose would not care
at all, while he would suffer bitterly." [3]

On this occasion it was torturing someone he had cared for, as
well as himself. In later instances with Mildred, however, it is Philip
alone who suffers. Again and again after being rejected by the wait-
ress, he returns. An example is the occasion where he is forced to
return to the tea shop after Mildred goes out with the German, Emil
Miller. He knows he is torturing himself to return to her, but he
goes.

Another example is the time that Philip flunks his biology
examination in medical school.

"It was tea-time, and he knew that a lot of men would be having
tea in the basement of the Medical School: those who had passed the
examination would be exultant, those who disliked him would look
at him with satisfaction, and the poor devils who had failed would
sympathise with him in order to receive sympathy. His instinct was
not to go near the hospital for a week, when the affair would be no
more thought of, but, because he hated so much to go just then, he

_____

[3] P. 90.

3

went: he wanted to inflict suffering upon himself. He forgot for the moment his maxim of life to follow his inclinations with due regard for the policeman round the corner; or, if he acted in accordance with it, there must have been some strange morbidity in his nature which made him take a grim pleasure in self-torture." [4]

This is the first clear statement that the author makes giving substance to this thought that Philip actually enjoys inflicting pain on himself. It is revealed again with Mildred and Griffiths when the three of them have gone out together.

"Then a strange desire to torture himself seized him, and he got up, saying he wanted to go and drink something. Mildred and Griffiths had never been alone together for a moment. He wanted to leave them by themselves.... He was throwing them together now to make the pain he suffered more intolerable.... They were enjoying themselves without him, and he was suffering, suffering.... he cursed himself for having left them alone, he had actually gone out of his way to enable them to arrange things." [5]

About this time in the book you are wondering what in the world impels Philip to do these things to himself. In each instance it seems that he alone is responsible for the unhappy incidents. But, is it Philip alone that is responsible? He seems to think that other agents may be at work upon him. Whatever is responsible, you certainly begin to think Philip a fool when the Mildred-Griffiths relationship is aided by him even more. Finally he suggests that Mildred go away with Griffiths using Philip's money.

------

[4] Pp. 356 f.

[5] Pp. 450-452.

4

"Now that he had made the suggestion he was sick with anguish, and yet the torture of it gave him a strange, subtle sensation. . . . Her objections made him insist, and yet he wanted her with all his heart to refuse him vehemently. . . . He shook his head, smiling, but with what agony in his heart!" [6]

This evidently is not enough self-torture for him. When Mildred tells him that Harry has refused the offer, he continues to persuade her.

"A devil seized Philip, a devil of self-torture which was always lurking within him, and, though with all his soul he wished that Griffiths and Mildred should not go away together, he could not help himself; he set himself to persuade Griffiths through her. . . . But he had a fiendish desire to break down their scruples, he wanted to know how abominably they could behave towards him; if he tempted them a little more they would yield, and he took a fierce joy at the thought of their dishonor. Though every word he spoke tortured him, he found in the torture a horrible delight." [7]

It seems that after torturing himself, Philip always goes through pangs of regret. But he does not give up. When Mildred goes to Griffiths with Philip's proposal, Philip immediately regrets the offer.

"He wished with all his heart that he had not made the horrible proposition to give them money; but now that he had made it he lacked the strength to go back on it, not on Mildred's account, but on his own. There was a morbid obstinacy in him which forced him to do the thing he had determined." [8]

---

[6] P. 463.

[7] Pp. 466 f.

[8] P. 468.

5

He debates whether to leave so that they cannot have the money. But his final decision is "Let them come and take the money, and he would know then to what depths of infamy it was possible for men to descend." [9]

This is one of the last concrete instances found in the book of Philip's self-torture. In the last part of the book, however, you begin to wonder if he is again succumbing to the tendency. When Sally thinks she is pregnant, Philip plans to give up his dreams of foreign travel and marry her.

"His wedding present to his wife would be all his high hopes. Self-sacrifice! Philip was uplifted by its beauty.... He wanted to see Sally's happiness when he made her his offer...." [10]

But when he finds that Sally is not pregnant and that there is no need for self-sacrifice, he makes an important discovery. "It was no self-sacrifice that had driven him to think of marrying, but the desire for a wife and a home and love...." [11] On this last occasion it seems that Philip has finally grown up. He at last realizes that it is not self-torture, but happiness that he wants.

The reasons for his earlier self-tortures may be revealed in his earlier immaturity. After the Mildred-Griffiths incident "It seemed to him that he was swayed by every light emotion.... He had no self-control.... it seemed to him rather that he was swayed by some power alien to and yet within himself.... He thought of what he was going to do and, when the time came to act, he was powerless in the grasp

---

[9] P. 469.

[10] P. 755.

[11] P. 759.

of instincts, emotions, he knew not what. He acted as though he were a machine driven by the two forces of his environment and his personality...." [12]

Perhaps this last statement is approaching the core of his difficulties. All through his life he is forced to struggle with his emotions. His handicap is a great source of difficulty to him, and causes him to withdraw. In his tendencies toward self-torture he realizes some feelings of satisfaction. It is interesting to wonder what a modern psychoanalyst would make of Philip's tendencies. They would undoubtedly be traced back to his first feelings of self-consciousness over his deformity. You can almost visualize Philip describing his early life, as he lies on a couch. When he finally gets to the period when he dimly remembers his dying mother feeling his crippled limb, the solution is found. The psychoanalyst will cry, "This is it."

Not being a psychoanalyst, it is a little more difficult for me to decide on the basic reason for Philip's repeated self-torture. The author himself seems to hint that it is due to the eternal conflict between his personality and his environment. That, combined with his deformity, may be the answer. At the end, however, he seems to have matured enough to overcome partially his tendencies. The book ends with a note of happiness, "the sun was shining." [13]

---

[12] P. 478.

[13] P. 760.

III

APPENDIX

A

A BRIEF LIST OF REFERENCE WORKS

One can learn the *principles* of research through the card catalog, the *Readers' Guide,* and the encyclopedia. It is important, too, to know how invaluable the reference librarian can be. With this equipment, anyone with access to a library can further his own education.

But there are innumerable reference works, not only for the general reader but for the students of special fields. Find your way around the reference room of your library. The reference librarian can guide you, if you have a special problem. A few reference works [1] are listed below, and space is left for you to add others you may wish to record.

BIBLIOGRAPHICAL GUIDES AND INDEXES

Readers' Guide to Periodical Literature. 1907-. (The standard work of reference to general periodicals. It gives author, title, and subject index to about 200 current American magazines.)

Poole's Index to Periodical Literature. 1802-1906. (A subject index to about 470 nineteenth-century American magazines. The *Readers' Guide* continues for the twentieth century.)

International Index to Periodicals. 1907-. (About 300 periodicals from various countries.)

Public Affairs Information Service. 1905-. (A valuable source for new developments in economics, political science, and sociology.)

Agricultural Index. 1916-. (A subject index to magazines and bulletins.)

Education Index. 1929-.

Engineering Index. 1884-.

---

[1] In documenting references to these works, be sure to supply details of edition, volume, date, etc., where needed.

Industrial Arts Index. 1913-. (Engineering, business, and trade periodicals, books, and pamphlets.)

Cumulative Book Index. (An author, title, and subject index which will supplement the card catalog if in future you wish to avail yourself of interlibrary loan.)

Mudge, Isadore Gilbert. *Guide to Reference Books.* (This directory will guide you to other reference books.)

New York Times Index. 1913-. (If you want to know what was in the news at a given date, this will tell you.)

Book Review Digest. 1905-. (If you want to know what reception a book had when it first came out, this will guide you.)

Bartlett, John. *Familiar Quotations.* (Quotations are arranged and traced to their source.)

Bartlett, John. *New and Complete Concordance or Verbal Index to Words, Phrases, & Passages in the Dramatic Works of Shakespeare with a Supplementary Concordance to the Poems.*

Hastings, James. *Dictionary of the Bible.* (This will help you find anything in the Bible.)

GENERAL INFORMATION

Encyclopaedia Britannica. (This is the standard work of general reference to almost every field.)

Encyclopedia Americana. (This is valued particularly for its articles on business, government, industry, politics, and science.)

New International Encyclopaedia. (This has concise, readable articles for quick reference.)

Oxford English Dictionary. (This is the historical dictionary of the English language.)

Dictionary of American English. (American words, different from British, in print before 1900.)

New Larned History for Ready Reference. (This is an alphabetical dictionary of universal history. It has many cross references.)

World Almanac and Book of Facts. 1868-. (A year book: events of the year in various fields.)

Information Please Almanac. 1947-. (An annual fact book, edited by John Kieran.)

Cambridge History of American Literature.

Cambridge History of English Literature.

Frazer, Sir James George. *Golden Bough.* (A study in magic and religion.)

Gayley, Charles Mills. *Classic Myths in English Literature and in Art.*
Grove, Sir George. *Grove's Dictionary of Music and Musicians.*

BIOGRAPHY

Dictionary of American Biography.
Who's Who in America. 1899-. (Published biennially about living Americans.)
Dictionary of National Biography. (Best general reference for British biographies.)
Who's Who. 1848-. (Published annually; mainly British.)
International Who's Who. 1936-. (Published annually.)

STYLE

Manual of Style (11th ed.). Chicago: University of Chicago Press, 1949. (For styling to publication this is a widely accepted authority and is the standard for many leading publishers.)

STUDENTS' NOTES

B

ILLUSTRATION OF NOTES TAKEN FROM BIBLIOGRAPHICAL GUIDES

Bibliographical description should always be checked at the source. While compiling a bibliography, however, the investigator must take temporary notes from bibliographical guides which are styled to their special purposes and which may contain data not needed by the investigator. He must extract the data he needs and style it to his purpose. It is a saving in the long run to have the temporary note as accurate and complete as possible. This is particularly true with reference to the supplementary bibliography.

1. The following illustrate a *Readers' Guide* entry and the investigator's note taken from it:

> SITWELL, Sir Osbert, 5th bart
> Aspiring ape; poem. Atlan 184:51 N '49

Sitwell, Sir Osbert

"Aspiring Ape," a poem

Atlantic Monthly, Vol. 184 (November, 1949), p. 51

---

2. The following illustrate the author, title, subject cards in the catalog, and the investigator's note taken from any of them:

Author card from the catalog:

589.91
L 64 y Lindegren, Carl Clarence, 1896–
      The yeast cell, its genetics and cytology. 1st ed. St. Louis, Educational Publishers, 1949.

      1 v. (various pagings) illus. 24 cm.

      Developed from a series of lectures given at the University of Washington, Seattle, in 1947.
      Bibliography: 7 p. at end.

      1. Yeast.   I. Title.

      QR151.L66   589.2361   49–11233*

      Library of Congress   [15]

Title card from the catalog:

589.91   The yeast cell, its genetics and
L 64 y   cytology.
      Lindegren, Carl Clarence, 1896–
      The yeast cell, its genetics and cytology. 1st ed. St. Louis, Educational Publishers, 1949.

      1 v. (various pagings) illus. 24 cm.

      Developed from a series of lectures given at the University of Washington, Seattle, in 1947.
      Bibliography: 7 p. at end.

      1. Yeast.   I. Title.

      QR151.L66   589.2361   49–11233*

      Library of Congress   [15]

Subject card from the catalog:

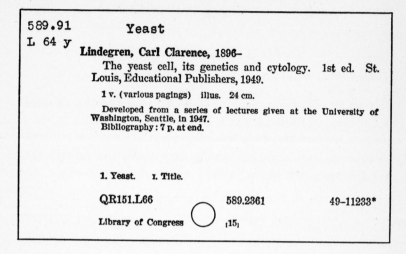

589.91
L 64 y

Yeast

Lindegren, Carl Clarence, 1896–
 The yeast cell, its genetics and cytology. 1st ed. St.
Louis, Educational Publishers, 1949.

 1 v. (various pagings) illus. 24 cm.

 Developed from a series of lectures given at the University of
Washington, Seattle, in 1947.
 Bibliography : 7 p. at end.

 1. Yeast. I. Title.

 QR151.L66   589.2361   49–11233*

 Library of Congress   [15]

Investigator's bibliographical note taken from any of the cards shown above:

589.91
L 64 y

Lindegren, Carl Clarence

The Yeast Cell, Its Genetics and Cytology

St. Louis: Educational Publishers, 1949

C

TYPICAL DATA NOTES

TOPLIFF'S NOTES FROM BUELL

In an article of some length,[1] Topliff found a section devoted to the oleo problem. From this section two paragraphs on a single page furnished for his investigation five substantial notes which were later scattered widely throughout the paper. The passages are given below, with Topliff's notes following:

Unfortunately for him [the American dairy farmer], the mere exclusion of foreign butter from this market has not prevented the rise of domestic substitutes such as oleomargarine. Now this substitute, while lacking some of the nutritive qualities of butter, looks like it when colored and sells for about half the price. Consequently, as times become harder, people buy more oleomargarine in relation to butter. Naturally the dairy farmer has become disturbed over this competition and has long endeavored to secure protection from it. The willingness of legislatures to come to his rescue is due to the fact that about half the oleomargarine is produced by the "wicked" packers. As early as 1886 Congress imposed a tax of two cents a pound on oleomargarine and imposed licenses upon its manufacture and sale. As a result of subsequent legislation, the federal government now taxes colored margarine ten cents a pound and uncolored margarine a quarter of a cent. No butter manufacturer is required to have a federal license to make butter; but the manufacturer of margarine must pay an annual license fee of $600 to Washington; wholesalers and retailers of colored margarine are taxed $480 and $48 respectively; while the similar tax on the uncolored product is $200 and $6 a year. The main purpose of this legislation is to safeguard against fraud, but this purpose could have been accomplished more effectively and honestly in a pure food and drug law. Undoubtedly this oleomargarine legislation has come to be regarded chiefly as a means of protecting the dairy farmer against internal competitors.

---

[1] R. L. Buell, "Death by Tariff," *Fortune*, Vol. 18, No. 2 (August, 1938), pp. 32-35, 88-90. The passages are quoted by permission of *Fortune* magazine.

[An omitted passage states that since cottonseed oil (instead of the Philippine cocoanut oil) has been used in margarine, the South has been on the side of margarine against the dairy industry.]

A more explosive statement of the southern view came in the Senate when an effort was made on April 15, 1938, to strike out the provision that had appeared in the appropriation bill since 1931, to the effect that none of the appropriation to the veterans' administration shall be expended for the purpose of oleomargarine except for cooking purposes. In attacking this provision, Senator "Cotton Ed" Smith asked, "Have we come to the point where we are applying a high protective tariff between industries within our country?" Senator Bankhead put in that "the people of Wisconsin ought to be satisfied to sell their great appealing commodity upon its merits in the free market of the country, without coming to Congress and asking for a congressional condemnation of one of the competitors which they must meet in the free market of the country." Senator Connally exploded, "I thought the war between the states was over in 1865." Despite these appeals from the South, the Senate voted to retain the oleomargarine embargo in the appropriation bill. For their part the southern representatives demanded compensation, not in the form of free trade but in increased protection against foreign competition with southern cottonseed oil! Notwithstanding these protectionist methods, consumption of oleomargarine increased from two hundred and sixty-five to three hundred and ninety million pounds between 1934 and 1936, the proportion of oleomargarine to creamery butter going up from 15 per cent to 24 per cent. To meet the situation, the dairymen are now lobbying for a new federal tax of five cents a pound on all margarine. It is hard to kill off competitors by protectionist means, but if the dairymen keep at it, they may succeed!

The type used in reproducing the following notes has been selected to suggest handwriting. Topliff's notes, taken in the library, were of course handwritten. The original notes show some instructive alterations, where the student had corrected the wording to bring out the meaning of the source more faithfully. This indicated that the student was taking the time, while at the source, to make a careful and accurate record.

The bibliographical note shows page reference only to the section relevant to the investigation.

Periodical Room   *3*

  Buell, R. L.

  "Death by Tariff."

  Fortune, Vol. XVIII, No. 2 (August, 1938), pp. 33-34.

  ["The dairy industry raises its defenses"]

The following became the eighth note in the paper (page 100).

Oleo & butter nutritional value   *3*

                               p. 34

  Oleo lacks some of the nutritive qualities of butter but looks like it when colored and sells for about half the price. Therefore, as times become harder people buy more oleo in relation to butter.

The following became the sixteenth and twentieth notes in the paper (page 103).

First laws   *3*

p. 34

In 1886 Congress imposed tax of 2¢ a pound on oleo and licenses for its manufacture and sale. Now: colored margarine 10¢ a pound, uncolored a quarter of a cent. No butter manufacturer has to have a federal license to make butter but oleo manufacturer pays $600 fee/year, wholesalers of colored $480, retailers of colored $48, uncolored $200 and $6. The main purpose of this legislation is to guard against fraud, but this aim could have been accomplished more effectively and honestly in a pure food and drug law. Has come to be regarded chiefly as means of protecting dairy farmer against internal competitors.

The following became the twenty-sixth note in the paper (page 106).

Interstate comments   *3*

p. 34

Comments in Senate concerned with the effort made on April 15, 1938, to strike out the provision that had been in the appropriation bill since 1931, requiring that none of the appropriation to the Veterans' Administration be spent for the buying of oleomargarine except for cooking use. Provision was voted to remain in the bill.

Sen. "Cotton Ed" Smith: "Have we come to the point where we are applying a high protective tariff between industries within our country?"

Sen. Connally: "I thought the war between the states was over in 1865."

(continued)

The following was incorporated with the preceding to form the twenty-sixth note in the paper.

Interstate comments (continued)   *3*

p. 34

    Sen. Bankhead: *"the people of Wisconsin ought to be satisfied to sell their great appealing commodity upon its merits in the free market of the country, without coming to Congress and asking for a congressional condemnation of one of the competitors which they must meet in the free market of the country."*

The following became the twenty-ninth note in the paper (page 107).

Increased consumption   *3*

p. 34

    "Notwithstanding these protectionist methods," oleomargarine consumption increased from 265,000,000 to 390,000,000 pounds between 1934 and 1936. Proportion of oleomargarine to creamery butter went up from 15 to 24%.

D

INTERLINEAR NOTES IN THE DRAFT

There are various methods of placing footnotes in a paper. The models in this text illustrate the most widely accepted form for the reader's copy. One variant, however, deserves particular attention.

The problem of adjusting the page can cause considerable difficulty in drafting a footnoted manuscript, particularly when revisions need to be inserted.

For this reason some prefer to place the footnotes interlinearly where they come in the text and thus to avoid the troublesome problem of determining the number of notes to a page. Printers and typists often prefer to receive manuscript with interlinear footnotes, and many approve of having all manuscript in this form. The following is part of the Ryan paper typed in this manner. Compare this with the reader's copy (pages 9 f.).

JOHN L. LEWIS'S COAL STRIKE

by John P. Ryan

Since November no man, except possibly the President, has had his name in the papers more often than John L. Lewis. The reason is that Mr. Lewis has had the members of his United Mine Workers Union out on one of their longest and most costly strikes. What are some of the reasons behind this strike that has caused Mr. Lewis's name to appear in print so much, and how will the differences be settled?

Mr. Lewis has several reasons for this long strike. As a recent issue of U.S. News and World Report reported, "John L. Lewis is not happy about his 1949 record of getting things for the miners of coal. . . . the miners have suffered sharp loss of income this year [1949] and have little to show in the way of added benefits for the year ahead." [1] Consequently, Mr. Lewis will first demand higher wages.

[1] "Whispers," U.S. News and World Report, Vol. 27, No. 20 (November 11, 1949), p. 68.

The pay of the miners, as a group, has increased as much as the pay of any other labor group, but the increased living costs have eaten most of these increases right up. This same magazine pointed out in another issue that the pay scales have risen from $9.05 per day to $14.05 per day, but that these increases have been met by increased living costs. [2]

[2] "High Cost of Strikes," U. S. News and World Report, Vol. 27, No. 16 (October 14, 1949), p. 11.

A second demand is for increased payment to the welfare fund. The fund was financed at the start solely by the operators, who paid a royalty of five cents a ton on coal, but the royalty was increased to twenty cents a ton. [3] Mr. Lewis has asked that since the fund is almost

[3] Ibid., p. 13.

defunct the royalties be raised to thirty cents a ton; also, that the board of trustees be changed, especially the representative for the operators.

Mr. Lewis has asked for other terms. These terms include a

E

BIBLIOGRAPHICAL ENTRY IN THE PAPER, WITH ILLUSTRATIONS NOT SHOWN IN THE MODELS

This is a manual of instruction rather than a manual of style. There is much inconsistency in the conventions of bibliographical entry. Where so many variants have acceptance, a text does not presume to impose a standard. A text presents a widely accepted variant suited to the needs of the student and readily adaptable to the individual preferences of instructors and editors. Whatever convention is adopted, it should be consistent and intelligible. The important thing is to describe the source so that the reader can find the page referred to.

For the sake of simplicity, this text suggests the following order: author, title, publisher or publication, and date of the *writing* referred to. Thus, if the *writing* is a selection included in a book by a different author, the secondary author becomes a part of the facts of publication, and the description might read thus:

[1] Sir James Jeans, "The Law of Gravitation," as quoted in Louise E. Rorabacher, Assignments in Exposition (New York: Harper & Bros., 1946), p. 173.

The procedure of this text suggests that the student begin by mastering the form of the footnote. In Assignment A, he follows his models and makes his descriptions from source. This is important. But it is not easy to get into the habit of following models and describing from source. Even with the best of care, one is likely to make oversights in mechanical details. For the sake of practice, it is advisable to make a fresh copy in the revision.

But once the footnote is mastered, it is comparatively easy to interpret other bibliographical entries. The *Readers' Guide* and the card catalog are styled to purposes different from those of formal writing. The bibliographical note card requires a slightly different form for ready reference. Finally one comes to the problem of setting up the bibliographical table in the formal report.

There is not much difference between the footnote and the entry in the appended bibliography. The footnote is a kind of parenthesis in the sentence structure of the text, and is punctuated and constructed accordingly. The place, publisher, and date of a book require parentheses to avoid awkwardness of construction when followed by page reference. They do not require parentheses when they close the note. The footnotes give the exact pages referred to in the discussion.

The bibliography gives the full page-span referred to in the *study*. The author's surname is placed first, and the tabular indenting of the line creates a pointing finger indicating the place of the entry in the alphabetical order of the bibliography as a whole. A period separates the author and, in the case of a book, the title and other main parts of the description.

When a paper has a bibliography, the place, publisher, and date of a book are generally omitted from the footnote. Otherwise, generally, the footnotes read as they would in a paper without a bibliography. This is illustrated in the Carson report.[1] There is, however, a growing acceptance of a more simplified economy, illustrated in the Gongwer report.[2] Here the bibliography lists the sources in full, and short forms are used throughout the footnotes.

In Gongwer's simplified convention, the short forms are given throughout the footnotes, since the full description is furnished by the appended bibliography. In Carson's more formal and as yet more widely accepted convention, the first

[1] Pp. 68 ff.
[2] Pp. 45 ff.

footnote to a magazine article gives the full bibliographical description; for a book the place, publisher, and date are omitted in the footnote, since they are furnished by the bibliography. In both conventions, later references to the same work employ the economies of the short forms.

Certain abbreviations are customary in footnotes and bibliographies. The models show the common ones. Particularly, words designating parts are abbreviated when combined with numbers. The following is a list of some of these abbreviations, with their plurals in parentheses:

p. (pp.) page
l. (ll.) line
vs. (vss.) verse
f. (ff.) and the page, line, or verse following
Vol. (Vols.) volume
No. (Nos.) number
chap. (chaps.) chapter
sec. (secs.) section
col. (cols.) column
Fig. (Figs.) figure
n. (nn.) footnote
ed. (eds.) edition

Proceeding from Assignment A, the footnote form becomes basic. It is what the *writer* uses most. (Once this form is mastered he can make his own adaptations.) Some of the footnote forms not shown in the models are illustrated below. Space is left for the student to add others he may wish to record.

Where a selection from one work is included by the editors of an anthology, Sanders' method of referring to Cannon [3] is adequate for the purpose. For a source study, however, the writer would if possible return to the original source, and the entry would appear thus:

[2] Walter Bradford Cannon, The Way of an Investigator (New York: W. W. Norton & Co., Inc., 1945), pp. 75 f.

[3] P. 11.

Place, publisher, and date require parentheses to avoid awkwardness of construction when page reference follows. They do not require parentheses when they end the note:

³ Walter Bradford Cannon, The Way of an Investigator, New York: W. W. Norton & Co., Inc., 1945.

When the pages referred to constitute a discrete section of the writing, this is usually indicated:

⁴ Walter Bradford Cannon, The Way of an Investigator, chap. vi, "Gains from Serendipity," pp. 68-78.

When details are taken here and there from an extended passage, *passim* is added to the page reference:

⁵ Ibid., pp. 69-74, passim.

When the writing described is an edition, it appears thus:

⁶ Theodore F. Gates and Austin Wright (eds.), College Prose (2nd ed.), Boston: D. C. Heath & Co., 1946.

A translation appears thus:

⁷ Fyodor Dostoyevsky, Crime and Punishment, trans. Constance Garnett, Modern Library edition.

Where there are more than three authors or editors it is customary to name only the first, with *et al.* (*et alii* is Latin for "and others") added:

⁸ David Lee Clark et al., Form and Style, p. 31.

When footnotes nine and ten appear on the same page, they should be spaced so that the footnotes are evenly indented:

⁹ Ibid., p. 6.
¹⁰ Ibid., p. 3.

When referring to Shakespeare, the reader needs the line to find the page. Where so many editions are available, it is rarely important to give the facts of publication. Neither does one ordinarily need Shakespeare's first name. Note also that *line* is not abbreviated here:

¹¹ Shakespeare, Hamlet, Act IV, scene 7, line 107.

Abbreviations are capitalized when they begin the footnote, according to the practice of *Modern Philology:*

[12] L. 108.

Bibliographical entries for public documents and government reports are particularly troublesome. Not only do they vary but sometimes they change, and the librarian has to reclassify. Each investigator must do the best he can with the copy at hand to get the author, the title, and the necessary facts of publication, as Hart has done. One document not in the field of agriculture is described according to the University of Chicago [4] style:

[13] U. S. Congress, Senate, Reorganization of the Post Office Dept., Hearing before Committee on Post Offices and Post Roads, U. S. Senate, 74th Cong., 1st Sess., on S. bill 1573, April 18, 1935 (Washington: Government Printing Office, 1935), p. 20.

An entry for a widely known yearbook might be as brief as the following:

[14] "Chronology," World Almanac, 1948, p. 753, col. 2.

The following describes a reference to a newspaper:

[15] Edwin L. James, "Pooling Plan of Paris Important at London," New York Times, May 14, 1950, p. E3, col. 7.

If no date is found, "n.d." is used:

[16] Gale Pedrick, A Manual of Heraldry, Philadelphia: J. B. Lippincott Co., n.d.

Magazines do not all have a "volume." When they do not, they may be referred to by date alone without parentheses. Yet, since it is easy for errors to slip in when dates are copied, the reader is more certain to find the right page if the number of the issue is also mentioned, with the date in parentheses:

[17] "Oleomargarine Faces New Attack," Business Week, No. 446 (March 19, 1938), pp. 26, 31-32.

---

[4] Kate L. Turabian, *A Manual for Writers of Dissertations* (Chicago, 1937), p. 26.

STUDENTS' NOTES

INDEX

139